HOW TO BE F***ABLE AT 90

Good Advice for All Ages

David Leddick

White Lake Press
Miami Beach

FIRST EDITION

Tables of Contents

Subsequent Diary Entries are followed by Diary Comments and then further followed by challenging Questions for you to answer after reviewing the answers of other people posed with the same question.

Foreword

To my amazement I was reading in the catalog for a Duane Michals show at the Morgan Library and I came across him saying in an interview exactly how I feel about life. "What if you could see pure energy?... In science, energy is not created or destroyed. Here's Duane alive, here's Duane dead. And when you die the energy in you is transformed into another package, that's all."

Duane is a very unusual artist, a photographer who then uses the photographs to communicate very individual, personal messages to the viewer. I worked with him in advertising. He has a magic no one else in the photography world has.

That is how I feel about life. We are in some enormous system of energy. We enter carrying it, spend our lives using that energy. Perhaps to make this world a better place. Perhaps to make it worse. Who knows? But in this 70, 80, 90 year visit we are on this beautiful globe, spending the time with other people. We can try to fully experience this time we spend here or we can do it a bit and then just sit about not using the life energy most of the time we are here.

This book is to encourage you to not just sit about. Now that more and more people are somehow having more and more years to spend on this "energy" visit, shouldn't we try to make our interactions with those around us as meaningful as possible? Shouldn't we feel and interact with the world around us as much as possible?

I awoke one morning and thought, "I must write something about what it is like to be approaching 90 years old. Everyone is living to be so much older. They need advice as to what is ahead of them. From someone who has been there. So they will know what to expect. What they can do to fight off what the world thinks being ninety is like."

I decided to do a daily diary. Even if it is only a page on occasional days it should be a book in some six months. Very likely sooner, as I plan to weave my thoughts and conclusions into the everyday events I will recount.

There will also be a series of questions to be answered by you to yourself. They may be deeply personal as far as you are concerned but the responses are only for you to read, mull and think about. I tested these on a mixed group of people and include their answers to let you find out what other people think.

Here goes.

Wednesday, July 31, 2019

It is a hottish day in Miami Beach. Being near the bay there was a nice breeze when I took the dogs out for their walk this morning. Sophie, my little chihuahua/dachshund mix and Baby, a beautiful mix of boxer and beagle is my guess. Sophie found under a garbage disposal unit some twelve years ago by my cabaret partner Andrew Sargent. He called and said, "I just found this little dog. What should I do with it?" I replied, "Since you're calling me I imagine you plan to bring it here." Which he did, and she has remained here since. The vet thought she was about two years old when found, which makes her now fourteen. She only likes her Dad. She's very hesitant to be friendly with the rest of the world.

Her sister Baby is now five and was tossed from a car one morning in front of the house where I lived on the Venetian Causeway. First she frolicked with the gardeners on the lawn and then came running into the house. Her smile and her affection for all others were already present. She has since grown into a very beautiful blonde. On walks she rushes to meet any new person or canine. In the night she sleeps lightly pressed against my body. Being rejected by her first owner as a puppy had no psychological impact on her. The people we meet walking always say she is the happiest dog in Miami Beach.

I immediately walk the dogs along the bayfront. They do not need the walk for toilet matters. We have large pee-pads in the house so they never "have to" take a walk. However, there will be mumbling and muttering if one sleeps in too long.

I follow up the walk and a bit of breakfast with twenty minutes of meditation in the morning also. I was a very persevering Zen student, commencing some fifty years ago. Perhaps a bit more. I attended the Zen Center in New York City each Thursday evening where those present meditated for two hours. With several interruptions and a short talk from the Abbott. In the question period one evening someone wanted to know that since there was no difference between men and woman in Zen studies, why did the women sit on one side of the meditation space and the men on the other? The Abbott smiled and answered, "Because there is no difference."

Who can resist a spiritual pursuit where one can be witty?

—

6

There were also weekend meditation retreats in the city center. Longer ones could be put in your schedule at the mountain retreat in the Catskill Mountains, north of the city. That was a full week of meditation commencing on a Friday evening and beginning at 7:00 A.M. and continuing through 9:00 P.M. for the following seven days. You actually had to arise at 5:00 A.M. to do your cleaning and maintenance duties and have breakfast. You were not allowed to look at anyone or speak to them at any time. There were stray cats sheltered in the basement of the large, very Asian Zen retreat. I cried every morning holding a cat. One of my duties was to feed them.

From time to time a small bell would ring and you could stand and meet the Abbott. He was the only person you were allowed to look at or speak to during the week. All the newer students always went to him as it was a chance to move about. My only memory of meeting with the Abbott, a youngish Zen Master from Japan, was telling him how painful my knees and feet were from the endless hours of sitting cross-legged on the mat. He said, "It goes away when you stand up, doesn't it?" I agreed that it did. He looked at me quizzically and said, "Well?"

I have continued my Zen practice, although I know that many of those I knew from the Zen center have not. I feel it pushes me into a kind of calm, central mental position each morning. I would not say that I have become any clearer as to why we are here. I do remember one other conversation with the Abbott after I had been doing an annual week-long meditation at the country retreat for some seven years. On a Thursday morning it became very clear to me that I was unimportant. When I reported that to the Abbott he said, "Now you're getting somewhere."

Knowing that I am very unimportant has actually been supportive for me. I have always pursued experiencing everything in life I wish to experience. Much more than security, fame or wealth or the things I think most people pursue. I will write much more about this as the diary progresses.

Diary Comment One

Admit it. Your waistline may have expanded. Your memory may have shrunk. But sex is still of interest. You thought it might fade, but it hasn't no matter how much you may have explored such activities as meditation or yoga.

I know this is not just uniquely in my own case as I pre-pandemically attended a yoga class regularly which was also well-attended by women ranging from 65 to the late 70s in age. I have become friendly with a good number of these ladies and they are quite open in discussing what is going on in their private lives.

They are for the most part single divorcees with a few widows mingled in also. Because of their yoga attendance all these ladies have slender, youthful bodies and are very physically supple. They can readily stand on their heads and fall into splits.

They are also very handy on the computer, making a lot of contacts with men who may be interested in meeting them socially. Again this is before the pandemic has closed everyone within their own home. Surprisingly a number of these lady friends are involved socially and sexually with men up to fifteen years their junior. One of them is being pursued by a much younger jazz musician who calls after finishing playing late into the night and insists on coming over to see her. She is open to these late-night visits, which frequently makes her unavailable for lunch.

All of this is just to point out that you may have been thinking about your sex life in terms of how it has been in previous years. This you must forget and move on. You may be attracting others and have no idea that you are. These others may be a good bit younger than you are. They may be of some other race. They may be of the same sex. They may be very much involved with someone else and thinking about you as a tempting addition to their private life.

You may even be passing time with people who spend some of their time in sexual threesomes, attend orgies, pick up strangers and all kinds of other things. You are now at a point in your life where you know about these kinds of activities and dismiss them as being of no interest. On the other hand it is completely within the realm of possibility that some of these things do ring some bells for you.

—

8

As for male acquaintances my having had some ten careers has left me with many contacts in many different milieu. Most of these have been phone contacts which fits into the pandemic lifestyle with no problem. Overall they seem to be shifting gears into a wider variety of sexual activities, seizing opportunities when they arise.

This includes someone who happens to be seated beside you at the theater, a female taxi driver (and from time to time a male), a neighbor in your apartment building, a teacher at an adult education class.

Overall men seem to be more open to unexpected sexual pop-ups. There is also the fact that single men with some credible income can be attractive to any number of women who will make themselves sexually available in interesting ways with the goal of a committed longtime relationship and marriage.

All of this is to make it clear that a sexual relationship may be established on some other basis than being sexually compelling. However that is not the direction in which this book is going. More and more there will be the explorations of what sexual involvement involves. Hopefully the advice offered will energize sexual relationships and keep them alive and thriving over long periods of time.

Thursday, August 1, 2019

This is a day, hectic with rain and much confusion about final documents for my move next month. By the end of the day we should have it sorted out. It may be possible to move at the end of next week. I'm going back into the building where I moved from, quite nearby. The same apartment as the one I owned, just below one floor.

It's a good apartment with great views of the bay, sizeable rooms and agreeable to the dogs. There's a nice balcony where they can be in the sun and move in and out of the apartment.

I thought I'd reveal a bit about my private life in today's entry. To justify the name of the book a bit. As I have passed through this life it's clear that both our body and our mind must be considered and cared for. Our bodies need contact with other bodies. We live in quite a puritanical society here in the United States. Much more than we realize. Having lived in France for many years I can compare the two societies. When a former Prime Minster dies and leaves not only a family but a mistress who has a daughter by him, no one in France is surprised. What would be a scandal in the U.S. is only news in France. He did not divorce his wife and re-marry. He handled his bodily needs by maintaining someone else in his life, a practice of some centuries in that country.

I had a boyfriend when I was four. He was always going to marry me when we grew up. My life as a gay person has never caused me any feelings of guilt. My mother brought up her four children to primarily be concerned with what they thought of others. What others thought of us didn't get much input.

There is a great deal more gay activity going on in this world than most people realize. Perhaps even more than when young women were much more involved with preserving their virginity until marriage. I always had a good deal of attention and did not sleep with other people just because they wanted to sleep with me. By the time I was in my twenties I was only interested in a real relationship with another man.

My first lover was someone I met while in the U.S. Navy as an officer. I served aboard an aircraft carrier and did 19 crossings of the Pacific Ocean. I was at Bikini Atoll for the hydrogen bomb tests and before leaving the service was attached to an admiral's staff. I saw a lot.

I think my first lover had very little attraction to other men. It was my (at least perceived) self-confidence that attracted him to me during the very chancy and dangerous operation at Bikini Atoll, I believe. He continued on to New York with me after both our service time concluded. He had yet to attend college so after a few months he returned to his home state. In college he fell in love with his French teacher and shortly thereafter married her. And there it ended between us. He was always quite uncomfortable talking to me after his marriage vows.

I was pretty much devastated at losing him but shortly pursued a dance career. Then advertising and several other adjunctive careers before becoming an author rather late in life. I had three more long-term lovers. The third with whom I am involved at the present time. I'll discuss this later in the diaries.

I do believe that your body requires the release of orgasm regularly and is best replenished with actual sexual activity. I think it helps fend off illness and helps keep your body healthy and resistant and also calms the mind. If there is another life after this one I think the orgasm is the experience that will let you have a hint of what that life might be like. One needs these transcendent experiences to keep the small grievances of life in perspective.

I read somewhere that if most couples put a small stone in a jar each time they had sex in the first year of their marriage and then took one out each time afterwards that they would never empty the jar. This is something to think about. I should add that I am not recommending a lot of extra-curricular fooling around. I am only recommending a good deal more experimentation and knowledgeability about where your partner might like to go sexually. We all grow and change sexually as we pass through life. Why not together? Your private life is your own concern and in no way needs to be lived to meet the consideration of others.

Diary Comment Two

Your body. Please. Don't throw in the towel. I think as people pass through their lifespan they come to a point where they must take some very decisive steps to hang onto what their body looks like. It is at that point when they either begin to diet, exercise, get a new kind of haircut, or they don't.

If they don't there is a very definite acceptance that no one is going to have sexual intercourse with them anymore unless it's some kind of duty. Or that other person may also have decided that personal attractiveness is something they are no longer going to concern themselves about. And you are the only sex available.

What I'm trying to explain here is that you don't want to simply assign yourself into the secondary category. For someone to truly have some desire for you it is important that you think equally well of yourself. You're worth it. You are. I think it's very important as you face the latter part of your life that you take steps to make it as interesting and as much fun as the earlier years were. Maybe even more so.

Now you know about things you would have liked to do. That you haven't done enough yet. Or perhaps at all. We all are filled with dreams and fantasies. So here are some suggestions as to how to get your body better prepared for the explorations you will soon embark upon.

1.

Are you overweight? Have you substituted sweets for the sweet stuff you really prefer to have in your life. This is a big American problem. Something like 40% of the population is obese. You see men walking down the street, stomachs protruding and you think, "Where in the heck is their penis?" What kind of penis would they have to have to sneak its way out from under all that avoir du pois and into someone else's body?

I also think that all that drooping weight may be their solution to just leaving the party altogether. If they are with a life partner this would be a great excuse for not having any kind of sex life. How could they? And if single it's a great way to avoid rejection. There's not going to be any coming close to this man.

You can eat less. Substitute liquids for solids. Have plenty of tea or coffee for the first meal of the day. Orange juice with additional Vitamin C tipped into it. Get that energy up without sugar pepping you up.

Only have one larger meal per day. At midday so you can burn off calories in the second half of the day. Load up on salads that are chock-a-block with shrimp, tuna, filling stuff that will not add many ounces to your frame but will make you feel filled up. No bread on the table. Maybe dessert but make it simple. One scoop of ice cream, not some kind of tottering pile of cheesecake.

In the evening eat as little as you can. Not a full meal. Maybe just some hamburger and oodles of carrots. Pile on the mustard and pickles. None of this adds weight. Eat a lot of mixed nuts for dessert, out of a jar so you can watch distracting TV. All of this works. You feel you've been eating a lot but you haven't had anything sweet. Sugar is addictive you know. After a few days you will stop feeling a need to eat cookies and cake and sweet rolls.

I have found that having a bowl of oatmeal first thing in the morning also gives you very regular and sizeable bowel movements the next morning. Unload as much food as you can every day.

2.

How about strengthening your body? Here's my advice if you find your buttocks are skidding southward. You want them up. Whoever you are, once you have your clothes off it's great when even sizeable buttocks don't droop.

It's not all that difficult to get 'em up; just walk up stairs whenever you can. Even in a large building you can walk up two flights and then take the elevator. Don't give in and take an elevator up one flight. Locate those stairs and walk up. I guarantee you, after one month you will see results. As will anyone else who is taking a look at your behind as you walk away, clothed or unclothed.

Here we go. Getting a grip on a renovated body. Not only is it good for your morale, it's very good for your health. As you head towards being effable as the years roll by, those years are going to extend also and your overall health will be much better. Come on. Isn't it great to have a future that looks even better than the past?

—

13

On the following page you will be asked the first of a series of questions. Ten people were pre-questioned and their answers are included here as a guide.

In the blank space that follows each question, you are to answer the question for yourself. In the print edition, you can even write it down. In the Ebook, just answer it mentally or write it on a piece of paper for future reference.

All of this is entirely private, of course, between you and yourself.

Question 1

What foreign country or countries would you like to visit where you've never gone before?

OTHER PEOPLE'S ANSWERS

1.   Although I have been in Europe several times I have never been to Paris. Primarily for shopping. A friend of mine told me you see things in shop windows in Paris you didn't know you wanted.
Female, 60s.

2.   The Andes Mountains. Everyone goes to the Alps. I want to go where other people haven't already been a lot.
Male, 60s.

3.   I think I would enjoy going to Morocco. For me it is the glamorous part of Africa.
Female, 50s, wife of No. 4

4.   For some years I have had the urge to go to Australia and make the trip across the entire country from Sydney on the East Coast to Perth in the distant West.
Male, 50s, husband of No. 3

5.   Buenos Aires calls out to me. I imagine it full of exotic, sexy people. Everyone ready to have fun.
Male, 40s.

6.   Am I a cliché? I want to go to Paris in France. I have never been to Europe but the French people I have met seem to be grown-up adults in many ways people in this country frequently are not.
Female, 40s.

7.   Italy. I want to go to Italy. Naples, I think. A kind of dangerous place.
Female, 40s.

8.   Two places. I have fantasies about two travel projects. One, I want to go across Russia from Leningrad all the way to the Chinese coast in the Far East. The long train trip. The people you would meet. And two, I wish to go to Shanghai. To me, it has always seemed the most fascinating place of places.
Male, 40s.

9.   I have been to Europe several times but I have never been to

---

15

Spain. Barcelona is where I want to go. I hear it's very edgy and modern.
Female, 30s.

10.   I think that one of the most international cities is right here in the U.S.A. That's Miami. Friends tell me people are there from Russia, China, Europe, all over. And they're all trim and run around without many clothes on. It's always summer. Yum.
Male, 30s.

Your answer to Question 1: What foreign country would you like to visit and why?

Friday, August 2, 2019

The high point of the day was lunch with my friends Leila and Jennifer at Balan's restaurant. It's sort of my club and office. Easily walkable, a pleasant terrace with tables set far enough apart where you aren't deluged with other people's conversations and very large umbrellas to protect everyone from our frequent tropical downfalls. Leila had called another friend of ours, Merle, and she joined us.

In conversation I said that I thought sleeping a lot helped conserve our strength and health as we wandered on through the accumulating years. Merle said, "You're a man. You can sleep. I have a lot of trouble. I just lie there in the night."

Late in the afternoon I worked out with my trainer Eddy and could see that I am getting stronger. I can do many of the exercises twenty times instead of fifteen. My niece Sarah had told me that my various problems like falling off my bike and having bronchitis were all first steps to a final decline. Since I did not seem to be declining from any of them, this was definitely not the end hovering. She did not call to inquire about my health for several weeks after that pronouncement.

Diary Comment Three

This comment is not going to be about sleeping well. I often tell people that my own mother told her children if they were having trouble with insomnia, "It doesn't matter if you are really sleeping or not as long as you lie there quietly. And you don't press your face into the pillow and make wrinkles." Of course a soon as you hear that you fall asleep immediately.

No, this comment will be about seduction. Do you really want to seduce someone or don't you? This can range from a person you have just newly met to someone you have slept with a great many times but you're in the mood and they're not. Here are some ideas for those of you who when it comes to sex you are ready to pursue your own selfish ends.

As an aside, rereading the diary entry that precedes this comment, it's clear that there is a certain amount of thinking about returning to this world, one way or another. In the return you would have the chance to do things you have not done successfully or haven't tried to do at all. I don't like this kind of thinking. You may have not fully accomplished some of your plans or hopes for yourself but you tried. You lived it. You did it. Instead of spending time thinking about vague possibilities of trying again in a second life, how about really going after things you want to do in the time you have here? Come on, let's pursue what we want!

You'd like to have sex with someone you have recently met. You are becoming better friends. Become friendly enough that you can suggest that you give this other person a massage. If they reject your offer, this is someone with little future for you, so that gives you one answer. If they accept, make a date at their place or yours.

Now you may have to face the fact that you know zilch about giving someone a massage. That is not a big problem. When you shampoo your hair, don't you rub your scalp thoroughly? It's just the same thing, except all over someone's body.

Get some body lotion. Put a large towel down on the bed you plan to massage them upon. They should only take their clothes off to their undergarments and lie face down on the bed. Arms by their sides, not overhead. No pillow.

It would be a good thing if they have had a shower shortly before, but if not, no problem. We're moving towards lots of tussling.

Start with their legs. First the calves. Apply your lotion. Just smooth it up and down on one calf. Then start squeezing the muscles. From below the knee squeeze and rub the muscles to loosen them down towards the ankle. Smooth them also. You can lift the leg, bending it at the knee to rub the leg on both sides.

After you do the other calf, do the feet. Your massage subject is going to love this. Even if the feet are knobby and pretty beaten up still rub across the arches with your thumb, push deeply into the sole, and run your fingers between the toes. Really loosen them up. Monsieur or Madame is going to like this a lot. It really does the most to relax the body you're working on. You can be sitting or kneeling on the bed or even slightly between the legs you're working on.

Once you've done from the knees down you will move to the upper thighs. Lotion, smoothing. Put your hands across the thighs as you've seen people squeeze dough. Perhaps you cook. You're pretty much there as far as massage is concerned.

As you approach the crotch you can spread the legs apart, more to massage thoroughly where the legs meet the buttocks. The degree to which the other person welcomes this tells you something.

The buttocks themselves. You can use both hands on both buttocks. Do not remove the underclothing but you can pull the top down a bit so as to actually touch the upper part of the buttocks as you squeeze the muscles. The buttocks are not as taut as the legs so you can really sink your fingers in and move them around to manipulate this part of the body. Your person being massaged may have an ample rear end. You can really dig in. It feels good for your massaged person.

Now you will do the back down to the waistline. You can decide if you can sit on the other person's buttocks or not as you do this. If not you can kneel beside the upper body. Move the arms up so they wing out to left and right. Start at the neck and upper shoulders. This will always be quite taut. Use your thumbs to rub up the lower neck. Squeeze those taut muscles across the shoulders. You can almost pinch them together to relax. Your massaged person should be beginning to really relax by now.

With your lotion smooth over the entire back and down to the waistline. Smooth over this area a good bit. This feels very good. You can interrupt yourself as you massage the back to massage arms

---

and hands. Smooth on lotion and rub and squeeze more gently. These muscles don't need a lot of effort on your part to relax as they are not used to support weight as have the muscles you have been massaging. If you are not seated on your massage objective you can move around from one side of their body to the other to massage the arms and hands.

The hands, like the feet, respond very well to massage. Just rub them gently when lotioned. You don't need to do the palms as much as simply spread the fingers and rub lotion. Well over the hands. You can place your own hand in the other person's hand, your fingers between their fingers.

Once you have massaged arms and hands you can return to the back and massage (rub) down to the waistline.

By this time you will be able to tell if you are heading somewhere sexual. If your massage subject is not opening their legs with any feeling of liking it and is resisting you with their muscles when you are working around the crotch area you can tell they do not wish to advance to something sexual with you.

However, if they seem to be welcoming your hands on their body you can move their legs apart and slip a hand up until it is enclosing the sexual area. If your massage partner is a man you should discover an erection. Massage it, also. From there you can turn your partner over and place your body on top of theirs. You are well on your way to having sex.

If your partner is a woman a finger or two should be welcome. If not, you will know the party is over. If so, again turn your partner over, now a romantic pairing has begun. Let it rip.

Tuesday, September 10, 2019

Today I had lunch with Wulf Treu. I call him Germany's Andy Warhol. He is a forty-ish tall blond man who escaped Eastern Germany as a teenager before the wall came down. He swam to an island mid-stream, thought he had escaped, was found and was returned home. Several tries later he made it, wandered around Europe, came to the United States, wound up in Miami.

Now he is becoming somewhat renowned for his original paintings, which make comment on the United States as seen from foreign eyes in a very semi-abstract way. The painting he gave me some years ago seems to be a man in high-heeled red boots. A more careful examination reveals a woman is beneath him, the red shoes not only on her feet but another pair on her hands. Her bosom protrudes forward and he is astride his female steed, crop in hand. A very bold painting that requires some examination to realize what you are looking at but like all major work by major talent, it looks great on the wall. Talking to him at lunch you realize that he is an observer in a world that has no background for him anywhere. He could just as easily have come from another planet.

A few nights ago I had dinner with my friend Alexis Caydam. I told him about an article I had read that morning in the *New York Times* about a man who had paid $34,000 to have his cat cloned when it died. First he buried it, then dug it up and put it in the fridge. Then had it cloned. There is now a kitten that is almost an exact replica, except for a missing black spot on the chin that the previous cat had had. Kitten doesn't have it. Owner is thrilled to have kitten.

One can see where this will lead. Children who die young will be cloned. Lovers will be cloned should they die unexpectedly. Many narcissistically-inclined people will have themselves cloned. Alexis said he would certainly want to be cloned so he could do the things he had wished to do and hadn't done. I told him that I had done everything I wished to do in this circuit.

He said, "But you might have a much more important dance career the second time." I said, "My body may be replicated but I am not going to have any repeats on what I did previously. I will know nothing about a previous life. We are here to fulfill ourselves as to what interests us. My clone may not have any of these interests. And certainly, he will be growing up in a completely different world."

For those of us here in a world that is increasingly different from the 20th century, we must try to do all those things that we perhaps haven't done. Go ahead, go to Paris. It remains very much what it always was. The French are very resistant to this new world descending upon them.

Those who wanted to learn to ice skate or roller skate, those things are quite accomplishable. You wanted to see the pyramids? They are still there, just as they always were. You want to go to China? You can certainly visit its ancient relics but you will be submerged in a hyper-modern world which has only come to exist in the past few decades.

Or perhaps it's the hyper-new that holds your fascination but also intimidates you a bit. Or more than a bit. Talking with a friend who is younger than I, he said he prefers to live mentally in the 20th century and not get used to cloning or transgender and all the other modern ways people are adapting themselves to this century. I told him nothing could guarantee more that he will be left behind as he ages, because he will be surrounded by people who do not have the prejudices or mindset of that time. He will have less to share with them all the time.

Diary Comment Four

When we realize how much the world around us is changing we will also realize that many of the ways we have learned to move forward into a sexual relationship with another person may no longer be useful.

For instance, letting your hand drop onto the crotch of the person seated next to you in the backseat of a car. The occasions when you are seated next to a person in the backseat of a car become fewer and fewer. You might ask about the possibilities in the backseat of a taxi. Except now you would very likely be in an Uber, and the present manner of driving in an Uber is that one person occupies the front seat with the driver.

A.
Dropping your hand into the backseat is very difficult and isn't likely to get anywhere. Dropping your hand into the driver's lap is not recommended at all as the result might be an accident, a very offended driver or being pushed out of the Uber vehicle somewhere you have no interest in being.

B.
Should we wish to return to the possibilities, if you think your sex potential partner is showing some interest in you the dropped hand may be met with an appreciative spreading of the legs and perhaps a hand upon your hand. If not, you can still say "Oh, please excuse me." As if you were simply trying to move over and misplaced your hand. If not, that misplaced hand may proceed to opening a fly or lifting a skirt. Almost certainly a reciprocal hand will arrive in your lap and very soon sexual parts will be explored and who knows? The whole thing may proceed to exchanged masturbation. Or if you are heading to one person's residence or the others, there can be some rapid re-buttoning and straightening of clothing until you arrive.

Question 2

What famous or well-known person would you like to meet? Why?

OTHER PEOPLE'S ANSWERS

1.   Meryl Streep. I just saw her movie "Laundromat." They film her like she really looks. She's brave.
Female, 60s.
2.   I would like to meet Elizabeth Warren. She is as intelligent as or more so than any of the other Democrat contenders and she's also an adult, attractive woman.
Male, 60s.
3.   LeBron James is my choice of a famous person I'd like to meet. I love basketball and this guy has got it all. Tall, mature, strong and he's got to be smart.
Female, 50s.
4.   I want to meet Ellen DeGeneres. Here's a real 21st century woman. She is who she is. No pretense. Nothing but up-front.
Male, 50s.
5.   My choice is Mayor Buttigieg. That little guy has a lot of guts. I'd be very happy if he was President.
Male, 40s.
6.   Diana Ross. Diana Ross. Diana Ross. Maybe the most beautiful and talented woman in the world in the last 100 years.
Female, 40s.
7.   My vote is for Adam Driver, the actor. Not really handsome but he's got force. I'd marry him in a minute.
Female, 40s.
8.   I am torn between Emmanuel Macron, the President of France, and Hilary Clinton. These people are leaders and manage to be attractive, well-dressed adults also. When a leader is sexy that is very, very rare.
Male, 40s.
9.   Some single young man who is running for some kind of state or national office. I want to marry someone who is involved.
Female, 30s.
10.   Saoirse Ronan. I hope I spelled her first name right. Such a good actress and such a good personality. She has great interviews.
Male, 30s.

Your answer to Question 2: What famous or well-known person would you like to meet? Why?

26

Wednesday, September 11, 2019

I went to yoga class this morning. I go two times a week. The Wednesday morning class is called a "restorative" class, which for me means we lay down most of the time. This is great. Yoga is very energetic. It is not a lot of woo-woo stuff.

The very strenuous classes in yoga are designed to give you an extremely supple body. This body when in meditative pose is far more receptive to your accumulating sensitivity to the world you find yourself in. I can certainly say that women's bodies are much suppler than men's and they advance more rapidly in the creation of these types of bodies. However, in the molding of the body there is no way to know what another person's interior world may be.

You quickly learn that yoga is not a competitive study. You are not there to be superior to another person. There are no leaders. We are there to make our bodies more receptive. That's it.

What I do notice, however, is that my female friends in the class rise from their strenuous efforts and are ready to rush right back into their lives. These are women somewhere between 65 and 75. They have excellent bodies. Their husbands have for the most part been lost to divorce. They are ready to meet new men and do new things.

One of my friends was married young at 19. By the age of 30 she had six children. These children are now all grown with families of their own and are distributed all over the United States. None of them are here in Miami.

My friend never had a "dating" period in her life. She was flung immediately into raising children. Now she has the time and interest and it is happening. A man in her apartment complex took an interest in her, they had a romance that was fully physical. Then he dropped her. She was devastated. We talked.

I told her, "Darling, you're only dating. They come. They go. They drop you. You drop them. Keep this in mind. You are having the experience you never had when you were younger." Now she has the idea. She encounters men online. They text. They exchange photos or sometimes not. They meet for a coffee. They perhaps have a lunch or a dinner. It can go a bit further or not.

It's very interesting. She is growing up in an area of her personality where she didn't have the opportunity to before. She has an excellent body and in addition is very intelligent and a lively conversationalist and social personality. Now at an age when many people have thrown in the towel she is exploring the world and learning.

She and I talked about this and confirmed for each other that in a successful relationship one party is usually manipulating the relationship and it is very important that the other person not be aware of it. The fact they do not have arguments is not that they are in complete agreement; it is that one person does not immediately voice their disagreement. They are there to demonstrate that their partner may not be entirely correct on the discussed subject. Perhaps days later. They do not mind picking up a wet towel or dirty socks. They are not raising a child. They have already done that. They are there to have a relationship.

They are also there because this relationship is physical. I once read in a Sam Shepard book, a porn-type novel written under the pseudonym of Phil Andros, this quote which I have always remembered: "What else is a body for? To meet and lie with another body, that's what."

I firmly believe that we have our bodies and we have our minds. We cannot be dismissive of what our body wishes to have happen. If this requires our maturing and learning some seductive techniques, so be it. You are not being overly manipulative. You are being adult.

I have seen this a good deal in my yoga classes. It is clear that as we become more mature, interaction between couples in a physical way is in no way something that just evaporates. I have given my friend who is now dating a notebook and pen. I told her to keep notes on every man she is meeting with and record the interaction. I told her this might readily become a book. If it does, you may read it someday.

Diary Comment Five

This comment five should probably be headed with the title "Would You Rather Have Sex or Have Dinner?" I've commented on this before. At some point as the years roll by you may decide that you are not going to be able to hang onto your body without a certain amount of effort and you are not willing to make that effort. Your attention then shifts to what you are going to eat.

This is a mistake if you look forward to the years ahead. There may be a whole lot of them and you are going to want to know younger people as they go by. You need to hang onto the appearance that makes you seem like a cohort to those younger people. You cannot lose yourself in whether to have apple pie or chocolate cake for dessert.

You may have already begun to enter that period of excess flesh hither and yon upon your body. Men, you may have that tummy protruding and beginning to descend. Ladies, your derrière and hips may be requiring larger and larger skirt sizes and make wearing shorts quite out of the question.

My take on all this is that if you hang onto your body to some degree it indicates your interest in others. You wish to know them. You wish to interact with them. You are interested in romantic relationships or you are interested in having your own relationship become more exotic and sexually profound as the years go by. As you read this book ask yourself if you have ever questioned the person with whom you're involved in a way this book is questioning you. If not, you have some work to do.

If on the other hand you are slipping away into a deep interest in what you are eating it indicates you are making more and more contact with yourself instead of with others. You are pleasing yourself. Exploring what foods are to be explored by yourself. Or what specific foods are to be indulged in repeatedly. You may be treating yourself very well. But it is diminishing your relationships with others. Now is the time to ask again, "Would you rather make bamboula or make lunch?"

My friends from my yoga class would join me I believe in urging you perhaps to skip lunch altogether.

Friday, September 13, 2019

Until I typed this I didn't realize that it was Friday the 13th. We will see what kind of thoughts or mishaps may occur. This morning I had a call from France just as I was finishing meditation. It was Casey Blondes. She is a long-time friend, an American living in France for many years, and someone whose mind and thoughts I find very compatible.

She had just returned to France from the States where she had attended a relative's wedding and said that observing the French, she felt they were a completely different kind of human being. She said the Americans aged badly, walked badly, and seemed quite un-individual. I told her that this may be the effect of living in a country of rigid morality where your primary concern was with what others thought of you, not what you thought of them. The French are the opposite.

I told her about the plumber in Pontlevoy, France, the village where I have a home. Pontlevoy is very near the river that was the demarcation line between Occupied France and Unoccupied France during World War II. At that time our plumber was young and fled through the Chateau Chenonceau, a nearby chateau that crosses the river Cher.

He joined the Underground and throughout the war carried messages and did what he could to resist the Germans. The townspeople of his home village, however, cooperated very thoroughly with the German occupiers. Their abbey became a German training school and was used to house many officers supervising the occupation. They all got along fine until the Germans had to flee back to their home country.

When our young man who was to become the village plumber then returned, he was an outcast. He alone had resisted. The villagers had cooperated. They did not accept his actions and were never friendly again. He did not care. They were wrong, he was right. The fact that they greatly outnumbered him did not bother him at all. He was only concerned with what he thought of them. He spoke out strongly about this and I admired him very much for it. When I was in the village and saw the older citizens meandering about I wondered what they had done to make the Germans feel at home during the war.

I, who always felt like an outsider growing up in rural Montague, Michigan, had no plan to remain there. After military service I went to New York City. And in New York you rarely met anyone who had been born there. It was a city made up of outsiders from all over the country who came to work in advertising, publishing, theater, Wall Street, and number of other professions that at the time only existed in New York. Now many cities offer opportunities in these fields.

I had lunch with my friend Andrew Delaplaine, who is involved in bringing a musical to Broadway about Louis Armstrong. Armstrong was the only one of the jazz greats who created a career that did not nosedive and end in distress. He married four times. His second wife seems to have managed him upwards into the established celebrity he became.

There have been a number of very successful Broadway shows about performers, using their music as the structure. With Louis Armstrong there is the same possibility. He is associated with many jazz-age classics, music which will be used to create the show.

What is interesting is that younger audiences might know these signature songs but are not familiar with the stars of the past who were involved with them. Andrew has a 40-year-old friend who isn't sure who Louis Armstrong was. For this reason the creation of the show has big potential, bringing a fascinating story to a public energized by important and familiar music. Evidently the show will be framed around Louis's four wives, each in a different period in the long and well-recorded Armstrong life.

Tomorrow I am going to an opening of artwork that revolves around the 1969 Stonewall resistance to the police in New York City. It was the first energizing of gay acceptance in society in the United States. This is another thing the French find amusing. They have long lived in a culture where what you do in your private life is entirely your own business. No one feels it is their duty to make you conform as long as it isn't interfering with their own life. They do enjoy observing the American culture and often refer to it in conversation as childish. Then apologize to me.

The show will be interesting as I lived immediately across the street from the Stonewall bar in Sheridan Square in Greenwich Village and was present at the police raid. It wasn't anywhere the big deal it has become historically. I remember thinking, "Oh, those queens are at it again."

I conclude today's thoughts with a note about a book I am currently reading, M.F.K. Fisher's final book, "Last House," a collection of diary entries and short stories. She was taken early on with certain writers, among them Brillat-Savarin. He only wrote one book late in his life in the 18th century, "The Physiology of Taste," about the importance and enjoyment of food. Fisher quotes someone who wrote about Brillat-Savarin's death. "He left the world like a satisfied diner leaving the banquet room."

Diary Comment Six

This diary entry finished with a comment on Brillat-Savarin, a famous commenter on his life in France in the 19th century. The phrase remarked that he left this life satisfied as though he had dined well.

I want to add here that feeling satisfied as though you have dined well doesn't necessarily refer to your having had a good meal. It's that of having no regrets. What you did satisfied you.

Elsewhere I have stated, probably repeatedly, that in my own life experience it is clear that our bodies and our minds both need to have satisfying experiences in order for us to feel that we have passed through this life fully and satisfactorily. Sex is part of that.

This entry is going to start with some direction to women who are in a relationship. This is some advice that I am sure you have had in the past. When you go to bed in the evening do not go with your hair up in curlers and your face plastered with night cream. Wait and do that a bit later.

Go to bed with the sense that something exciting and different may happen tonight, even if you have been to bed with this person many times. With sex there is always that possibility of something surprising that suddenly emerges. Both from your partner and yourself. So, please, don't go to bed already preparing for the next day and planning to just skip over the night. You might even comb your hair and wash your face and check your body odor.

As I write these comments I await some flair of insight from my subconscious to invigorate each comment and the one for today came to me in my half-sleep just before arising. If you think that perhaps your male partner's penis could be a bit larger for you to enjoy it more, how about investing in a strap-on? Easy to do on your computer.

Then, whether you are a female-male couple, female-female couple or male-male couple you have some new explorations ahead of you.

Female-male can just be adding a replacement on his part, or maybe Madame straps it on and fools around with Monsieur. He might like a bit of pushing and pulling administered by the lady involved. Between the thighs the way the Greeks used to do it long ago. Or maybe a bit of a try from behind. Let the lady be the guy.

Hmmmm. New worlds open before us.

Two women can of course take some turns and see what kind of dimensions may develop in their relationship with each other. And of course, with two men, tackling some new larger dimensions will be an interesting experience without any threat to their relationship. It beats a threesome, which always winds up with one of the three being the onlooker.

This is today's contribution from my subconscious. Things that I have tucked away, probably thought I have forgotten and then when I need some research, my subconscious steps up. I am convinced that none of us have forgotten anything. It's all there. Just don't be surprised when it pops up.

Question 3

Are you finding yourself meeting fewer people you want to know? Are you doing anything about this? What?

OTHER PEOPLE'S ANSWERS

1.   Definitely. They probably think I'm boring. I have started studying Spanish, just to meet new people of lots of different ages and backgrounds.
Female, 60s.

2.   I started working out at the gym with a trainer. I get good energy there with other people exercising.
Male, 60s.

3.   Five other women are taking a writing class together with me. It's good because we talk about what we're writing about. Our own lives, of course.
Female, 50s.

4.   Not really. I play golf and lots of guys there of different ages and more women lately. Really athletic women.
Male, 50s.

5.   Your friends start repeating themselves as they get a little older so I am taking an English class at the local college. A lot of younger students but it's good to know another generation.
Male, 40s.

6.   Not fewer but newer. I need to meet some younger folks that's for sure. I could help out at a homeless food center near me on weekends.
Female, 40s.

7.   I'm studying fashion design right now full-time. Very interesting people. It's changing a lot.
Female, 40s.

8.   I have a good voice and I am considering studying singing with a vocal coach. Maybe I can sing in the local club. Opera? Is this a fantasy? I love it.
Male, 40s.

9.   I should meet some different people. I am going to start taking a modern dance class at the dance school near me.

Female, 30s.

10.   Tennis. I am going to play more tennis. I'm not bad and I
don't know anyone who plays tennis. It will be good.

Male, 30s.

Your answer to Question 3: Are you finding yourself meeting fewer people you want to know? Are you doing anything about this? What?

Tuesday, October 1, 2019

Autumn is upon us but here in Miami Beach that means very little. A bit breezier. That is all. I have been working on so many projects that I have not had time to have lunch with friends. So I think I'll just write about what I'm thinking about today. I think it's pertinent in the process of moving forward with one's life.

In moving from one apartment to another very recently I'm coming across possessions I have not given much thought to of late and giving many to others. In my library I'm coming across books that I haven't read in some time and have been doing some re-reading. Among them has been my friend Steven Pressfield's major book "The War of Art." This book is about overcoming the blocks that keep you from being creative. Particularly writing but also painting, music, and dancing. It's an excellent book but as I read it I realized that my art has not been writing but when I was trying to have a career as a dancer. I had the necessary love of the art and had the right body and musicality. I just started too late. And I think for a dancer, you don't really block your own career from a lack of self-confidence as perhaps in other fields, as you must go to class every day if you consider yourself on the way to a profession. Class itself is a great daily experience. You feel yourself deeply connected to a centuries-old training, each class beginning at the barre demanding rigid repetition of specific exercises in order to create the body you need. Then moving on to expression through movement as the class moves to the center of the room and faces the mirrors. You can't pretend something is happening that is not as you must regard yourself in the mirror at all times.

Doing this at the old Metropolitan Opera where all hallways were lined with large trunks containing costumes from productions of many years ago, largely marked upon each trunk, made you feel that you're evolving from deeply-based tradition. It was great.

Unfortunately it became clear to me after some years of training and actually working (I was tall and that was always in great demand) that I was never going to become a star or even a principal dancer. I would work in the corps de ballet if I was lucky and early in my thirties have to escape to teaching. I saw it all around me. Students were arriving from their late teens and in a few years those bodies could execute the required steps faster, jump higher, and

---

38

project more vitality and charm than the older dancers. Only the stars survived because their acting in lead roles in major ballets like "Swan Lake" and "Coppélia" made them unique and important. So I left.

After that my career was in advertising. I still went to dance class after work every day. There, for an hour and a half I really lived as the music and movement fulfilled me. I realized that I could only feel really alive about an hour and a half a day and ballet did that for me. The other twenty-two and a half hours would be filled with sleep, eating and a job. The job was just to pay bills, it had nothing to do with being fulfilled. My ballet class did that part.

I was working on the Revlon account at Grey Advertising. The Revlon people were monsters. I became the creative director and we did very noteworthy advertising for them, winning many awards and a lot of attention. Never in my twenty years with Revlon did anyone in their offices ever say that anything was good or that they liked it. They did heap abuse and disgust and rejection upon the advertising agency creative people on a daily basis. I always told my staff, "Leave your ego behind here at the office. What you hear at the client has nothing to do with the quality of your work. It is just the way they interact with others." The big plus was that they had mountains of money and would green-light a television commercial for $100,000 when no one else in the business was spending more than $20,000. We then departed and shot TV commercials in the Alps, in the Loire Valley in France, in the Mediterranean. That was major league and only they did it, to major impact and big profits.

When I decided to depart from that and begin writing, I never had any problem just sitting down and doing it. This wasn't the art that made me be concerned for my talent, expertise, imagination, etc. That had been ballet. My writing was just professionalism. I sold my first book, "My Worst Date," to a publisher without even having an agent. It had a good and pretty shocking story and sold very well. I did quite a few more for my publisher. It never occurred to me to be concerned about other people's opinions of my work. Once in a while I'd get a bad review and I'd think, "That's one person. That's not the public."

After awhile, as I was approaching the age when most people think of retiring, I was asked to work in a local musical in Miami Beach, where I had gone because I love the eternal summer of South Florida. I was an older advice-giving personality in the show but I

—

told the producers I had to have a musical number. Strangely enough I found I had a pretty good singing voice and from that show I moved on and began to create cabaret shows for myself and others. Again, I didn't seem to have any trouble writing and performing and I certainly wasn't concerned about what other people thought. I was having a very good time with much younger people and the audiences were having just as good a time as I was. Having a good time communicates itself. Self-confidence I think comes from relishing what you are doing. People like it. They want to see more of you.

Diary Comment Seven

"Self-confidence comes from relishing what you are doing." This is the final comment in this diary entry. It's something to think about when applied to sex with someone else.

Many times in this book I have said to the reader that it is preferable to only think about what you think of others. You can consider what other people think of you, but that is not the structure upon which one should build a life.

Other people's judgment of you is based in our culture primarily upon how much money you make, then how famous you are, then perhaps your family connections and perhaps finally your appearance. The more of a cliché you are the more you will be approved. And then what? Perhaps you are a cliché and all this will be fine. But chances are that you are not. That you are one of a kind. That you have desires and hopes for life experiences as you pass through your time on the globe. And that is where sex comes in.

Returning to the opening phrase. In sex, as in everything else, self-confidence always causes a positive reaction from others. And that is based largely on your self-knowledge that you are doing what you want to do and feeling fulfilled and very satisfied while you are doing it.

And so with sex. You may feel self-confident because you are doing exactly what you want to do. You are on top. You are on the bottom. You are talking out the window to an acquaintance while your partner is doubled over just beneath the windowsill (this has happened), whatever you are doing you are leading the way.

But there is also the counterpart to this. The other person is being fulfilled sexually and you are the one that is creating the circumstances and making it happen. Someone else being very fulfilled sexually with you can also be a sexually fulfilling experience. And this is not to say that you cannot have a sex life that occurs on both sides of this fence. You can.

Most importantly, whatever you do, however you are doing it, your self-confidence is what others will find appealing. It's this quality of yours that they wish to share.

Thursday, October 3, 2019

A very rowdy day, many phone calls from people from one end of the country to the other. Careers seem to be moving in many directions for many people.

Looking through my notes for this book this afternoon I found a list titled "What's Important to You?" One of those "Let's be honest with ourselves" moments. More and more as I get older it becomes clear to me how people react to one another. We like to think that we become more mature but I think in fact we become more simple. It's clear how we really function and we don't waste time with the things that have not been satisfactory in our interaction with life and others.

As for my list of things that are important to me, here goes:

1. My face.
2. My hair.
3. My body.
4. My clothes.
5. My art and furniture.
6. Literature.

I added the note "If you have all of that under control the rest takes care of itself."

When I look at the list it seems to be the order in which other people perceive you. With the exception of "Literature." I think from very early in my life I realized that you must present yourself at your best to the world. In that way you have done everything you can to get a good reaction. How they actually do react is their business and you don't have to concern yourself. There is nothing more that you can do about it. Literature is your interaction with how other people perceive the world they are living in.

As for my list, I think your face is your primary concern in your interaction with other people. I see so many people whose personality has been lost beneath sagging skin and many wrinkles. Now you are going to tell me that nothing can be done about this. Untrue. When you would spend more on a new car than a new face you have your priorities wrong. Someone might like your car but not necessarily like you. A facelift is scorned in the United States as if it were some kind of mask. Actually a good facelift only takes you back ten years. And that is quite enough. I have been lifted three times and my friends do not even notice. They say things like, "You're looking rested." The big difference is that you are immediately back in the mix. People want to know you. You get invitations. Young people want to sleep with you. Hello. Maybe it isn't you. Maybe it's better than you.

Your hair. For women perhaps just pulling it back into a neat ponytail or chignon may work. For me, it's much more of a problem. The current vogue for shaving the heard completely is addressing the problem and I don't think you may very well look better with a shaved head than a large bald spot or drastically receding hairline. But earlier on you might have tried to fight all that by standing on your head regularly and getting a hand massager to work your head over when hair begins to go. Both things work at hanging onto your hair. Your scalp is the thinnest layer of flesh on your body. Your heart has difficulty pumping blood through it as you age. You have to give it some assistance. That's how it works.

Then there's your body. If you just can't make yourself exercise and control your eating, you will have to throw in the towel. Forty percent of the population of the United States is obese. What does this have to say about people not wanting to have sex? I know I repeat myself about this being a much more puritanical country than most others. We don't think so because we are a very large country and we don't see a lot of variation. At any rate, if you're planning and wanting to have sex you have to bring something to the party, even if you have been married for some time.

Your clothes. You don't have to have a lot of them but they should make you look better. I leaf through the current Vogue magazine and wonder why any woman would wear most of the clothes shown there. They do not make you look better. They seem to be designed to make you look the center of attention or to try to smuggle your overweight body through the streets with a minimum of attention.

For both men and women, pay attention to your shoulders. If you are wearing tailoring, pay good money to have the jacket well-tailored. That alone gets you off on the right foot with others. The jacket seems to be on the skids, however. So then you have to concentrate on the overall fit of whatever you are wearing on your upper body. A very ancient rule, which I believe lives on, is that you need white around your face. It throws the light upwards. For men,

---

even a white sports shirt will do the job for you. For women, a small light scarf can be a substitute.

As for colors, we have all seen black move to the forefront. It conceals bodily problems well and leaves the whole subject of what you are wearing to be ignored. For myself, I think navy blue is a worthy substitute and still leaves you with a slight edge of being dressed smartly. This goes for both men and women. Brown is never to be preferred over navy blue or black. No one looks better in brown. Well, maybe furs.

Which brings us to the art and furniture in your home. They are there not to impress others or make a good impression. You can always entertain someone in a restaurant. And if they are there to sleep with you they're not going to pay a lot of attention to your couch. Your art and furniture are to provide pleasure and reassurance to you. Each time you pass a painting or print on your wall you have that little flair of pleasure that adds something to your day and life. Your couch and side chairs welcome you. Your antique table or desk may remind you of your family or past. Or remind you of a family or past you would like to have had.

Finally there is literature, to which there is no end. There will always be something new you wish to read. Some additional history on people or events from the past you would like to know more about. Or new writers with new points of view about events that have happened to you. So interesting to think about these events in new ways. The great thing about literature is writers always have something more to add to what you know about life. So life continues on without stopping to be interesting. Great, huh?

Diary Comment Eight

As I read this diary entry it certainly sounded very self-centered. I think it could be rescued a bit by adding that the list of things that I think are important are things that I can do something about. As for politics, I will always vote. I contribute a good bit to charities, particularly the one for hare-lipped children. One modest $25.00 contribution can help give a child an entirely different life. And here we are again.

Now, how about considering our lives as they are here in the midst of the great Pandemic. Very isolated if you are smart, even if it is not being imposed. Isolated with other people in many cases.

In some of the reports I've read there are people who find themselves isolated with an ex. That could be a spouse, or lover I suppose. In that situation, it undoubtedly becomes quickly apparent why this is your ex. Very difficult as you really don't want to find yourself slipping into having a sex life with this ex. And yet, and yet. This I think may be one of the most difficult situations people endured during this Pandemic when we look back upon it.

Also it is to be noted that as the Pandemic appeared in the large Chinese city where it first came into light, Wuhan, the divorce rate soared. Marriage is not a simple kind of thing. It's true a partner of yours should certainly continue to be sexually stimulating and yet on the other hand that partner may not have the qualities of a best friend. So being face-to-face all the time you aren't sleeping can certainly become very heavy going.

Which brings us to the certain Pandemic result of a lot of divorces and certainly a lot of re-couplings. So what perhaps could be a plan to make another round consistently sexy? Even while hopefully you are not in each other's presence an undue amount of time.

This is what my subconscious came up with today. Art. You need physical representation in your home. This, of course, is assuming you don't have children and teenagers in your home with you.

In my bedroom I have a rather gigantic painting of a nude male posing for a painter while looking at his reflection in an equally large mirror. We see his backside, in the mirror we see his front side and behind that we see reflected the painter himself at his easel. We don't see what he is painting but it is a self-portrait of the artist who created this large work.

Friends who may occasionally pass through my bedroom to use the bathroom are always very startled by this piece. It is art beyond any question. But it is equally a reminder of the beauty of the human body. The energy it exudes. The energy that invades your life from it.

In my living room, among other paintings and portraits, I also have bronze nudes: male and female. They are both antique and very excellent works I brought with me at different occasions from Europe. They too put a little extra zing in the world around me. As with all the art you may have each time you glance at it, pass it, notice it , you find yourself getting a little boost from color, shape, beauty, memory. As with sex itself, you need this. It keeps you aware of what is important in your life. And perhaps keeps you from eating too much.

Question 4

If you could have dinner with any infamous person, living or from the past, who would it be? Why?

OTHER PEOPLE'S ANSWERS

1.   How about Catherine the Great of Russia? A little German princess who married the crazed czar or Russia who died young. There she was for many, many years surrounded by people she wasn't sure she could trust. We could compare notes.
Female, 60s.

2.   Definitely Robert E. Lee, the general who led the forces of the South against the North. I've always wondered what he thought he was doing. Good-looking, smart, a better general than anybody in the North. Defending slavery. What could he say?
Male, 60s.

3.   Gypsy Rose Lee. Was she infamous? She certainly had a bad reputation and her mother launched her in that career. Her younger sister went into the movies. I don't think Gypsy slept around a lot. I'd like to ask her.
Female, 50s.

4.   I don't know that I'd want to have dinner with Al Capone, but I'd like to talk to him just to see what a guy is like who was responsible for killing so many people. Anybody who got in his way. I kind of know the feeling.
Male, 50s.

5.   Being gay I would like to have met Lord Alfred Douglas, the young blond aristocrat that Oscar Wilde loved. What did he think of the whole mess when Wilde sued Douglas' father for saying he was homosexual? Then Wilde's career was ruined and they ran off to Europe and before long Oscar Wilde died in a cheap hotel in Paris. I've seen that hotel. Whatever happened to Douglas I wonder?
Male, 40s.

6.   I'd have loved to have met Josephine Baker. There she was, young, black, dancing at the Folies Begrère in a string of bananas. I'm not black but I have the same first name. She had both male and female lovers so I might have had a chance with her.
Female, 40s.

47

7.   How about Monica Lewinsky, who got under the desk to give Bill Clinton a blowjob? She's kind of famous now. For a young girl of that period she was pretty casual. Now that I'm a woman you have to think about how women used to be very careful about their reputations.
Female, 40s.

8.   The train robbers Jesse James and his brother Frank. I just saw a photo of the two of them. The famous one, Jesse, was young and very pretty. Girlish. I'd love to know what was going on in those days.
Male, 40s.

9.   I want to meet the Hollywood actress Bella Thorne who has a boyfriend, then a girlfriend, then back to another boyfriend.
Female, 30s.

10.   Hard to say that there is much difference between famous and infamous these days. Mick Jagger could be a good choice. He doesn't seem to care what anyone thinks of him. Would he ever talk?
Male, 30s.

Your answer to Question 4: If you could have dinner with any infamous person, living or past, who would it be? Why?

Tuesday, October 8, 2019

Today it poured with rain, several times. Between lengthy downfalls I had lunch with my friend David Bolding.

We talked a lot about David's private life. He often goes to a popular bar very near where I live and asked me why he never sees me there. I told him I wasn't trying to meet anyone. I've heard the expression, "He always chooses buds that will never bloom." I don't know if this is the case but I do think he will not let himself fall hopelessly in love with someone and accept where that situation might lead. He's smart, he's amusing, and he's in good shape. I am going to talk to friends and see whom we might guide into his path.

I think we all have destinies and impulsively moving forward is how we pursue them. If we hold back and don't take what looks like a chance we may just be putting our destinies on hold. And may have to return to this life a number of times until we work up the nerve to fling ourselves forward.

Today I plan to go through my notes for this book and just record the snatches of conversation I have heard on the street and recorded. These are indications of other people and their destinies heading off in directions you will never have presented to you. So interesting.

"I have a boyfriend in California, which is where I think all boyfriends should be."

"Everywhere I want to go I can't. It's like Boston."

"He was sort of strap-on Butch."

"With all these new diseases I don't French kiss anyone anymore. Not even a member of my own family."

"He's German. I never know whether I'm supposed to take out the trash or invade Poland."

"I was having a severe depression and trying to fuck my way out of it."

"I've always gotten everything I wanted and I've tried to be a good sport about it."

(Heard in back of a theater) "Sorry? What do you mean you're sorry? You peed all over my girl."

Diary Comment Nine

My takeaway from this diary entry is, "Don't be too strict with yourself as you fulfill your destiny." Yes, you may be heading in a direction with your life that is pretty much what you had in mind. But you may be observing some self-served rules and regulations that don't need to be as rigid as you make them.

For instance, when you go to the movies. And I think that despite the inroads made by the Pandemic we will once again be going to the movies. If you are with someone who is a present or potential sex partner take your seats in the most isolated part of the theater you can find.

When you are seated and have consumed whatever popcorn or other eats you may have purchased and the movie isn't holding your attention particularly, you might try a bit of public masturbation. I want to add here that even if this never gets off the ground the other person is going to be impressed with your audacity. It is not going to make them get up and leave the theater. And if they do it's just as well.

However chances are excellent that a bit of zipdown or flip up is going to welcome your wandering hand. In the hometown where I was brought up it was well known that the back row on the left (as you faced the screen) was where this kind of activity was pursued.

I should also add that you would do well to always venture forth with a large handkerchief handy. To mop up all soggy results. You yourself may be drawn into this kind of sexy playing so you could surprise your partner by not be wearing any underwear. Perhaps you should be having more than one handkerchief in your possession.

As you leave the theater you may well be wondering what you were doing carrying on like that in public. But it will add a dash of daring and surprise to the other person's comprehension of who you are, what you're like, and what may be coming next.

One of my friends once confided in me that they had been drawn into a stand-alone telephone booth (this is before the days of omnipresent cellphones) and proceeded to have sex in the booth on a relatively deserted street. But not entirely. Passersby probably said to themselves, "Oh, they're just smooching." I was never told if it was raining slightly or not. That would explain a lot.

Sunday, October 13, 2019

I started with an hour and a half yoga class this morning. It was largely devoted to twisting our bodies from one side to the other while standing, seated, standing with one foot on a chair, seated on the chair with one foot squeezed up beside your crotch and several other odd body positions. We did enough twisting and turning to give me an 18 inch waist. Now, while I write this I am much more aware of the backs of my thighs, which feel as though they were torn asunder. The interesting thing about yoga is that while you think you are working on your waistline you may actually be marching your body through your hip sockets relating to your upper legs. I don't think many non-yogaites realize how physically demanding it is. The teacher even suggested in talking to us this morning that there may be some students there who are only trying to firm and enlarge their buttocks. As you grow older it is somewhat reassuring that among your other yoga benefits, you may be avoiding a fat ass.

My niece associates with a number of civic groups and is becoming well known around town. Our family heritage was to have little concern for what others thought of you and to only be concerned with what you thought of them. This serves her well socially as she is relaxed, interested in talking to the people she meets and an amusing conversationalist. At lunch we met my friend Jennifer and she exchanged points of view on the various local personalities running for city administration positions in the looming elections. As they talked it occurred to me that as one matures more and more, involving oneself in civic activities is a great way to continue adding new acquaintances.

As we age, the people we know become fewer. They die, they move, they aren't interested in socializing anymore. If you are going to remain in the swim of things you have to move into areas where you have not been before. You can study a language, go to a college class of adult education, involve yourself in political actions, and choose a charity to help out around town. If your primary reason is to meet new people, there is nothing wrong with that. You are contributing, whatever your motivation may be.

If romance is your underlying goal, or sex, or whatever, that's okay also. It's very important for your overall health and your overall mental wellbeing that you have social contacts. In this new century they can range over age groups and social worlds that they did not in the previous century. The great thing about yoga is that your brain shifts as well as your body. It makes leaving the past behind much easier.

Diary Comment Ten

This diary entry ended once again reverberating upon the subject of sex life. In this entry my subconscious has suggested to me that we take a peek at where you are as well as what you are doing.

If you are sexually involved with someone…married, lovers, just beginning …place can be important. They may very well be drawn to you because of what you add to their life. And what you add to their life may be the places you are with them.

Many people think about the places they should like to go, things they would like to see, but they don't get up enough energy to actually add this to their life experience. This is where you come in.

Go somewhere sexy. Like Miami. Or particularly Miami Beach. It is always summer there. The beach is large and sprawling and inviting. The mostly-pedestrian Lincoln Road stretches from the bay to the Atlantic Ocean. With the current Pandemic this large sprawling, auto-free street is empty. Normally it is lined with appealing stores and m any restaurants, all of them with large terraces in front of them.

As you lunch aspiring models, foreign visitors, very good-looking locals pass by. They are all minimally dressed. Even in the Pandemic very exposed buttocks are everywhere on the young women. The men also are usually unshirted with their pants or shorts dangerously lowered. This is the kind of world to visit when you want the atmosphere to sink into your own private life.

Other sexy places can be an island in the Caribbean. Or Panama, where the great canal seems to draw many visitors. Somehow the sight of very large ships being raised and lowered rapidly as they are packed into a tight canal is very emotional. This is the only place on the planet this is happening.

If you have the money, try a visit to Buenos Aires in Argentina. A large city with an energy in the air. A city North Americans know nothing about. It's jammed with night clubs, bars, glamorous stores. In this very large, very different city you feel like a different person. This is not a major tourist destination.

How about Naples in Italy, if you have the wherewithal? Also not very touristed, with an edge of danger to it that makes you feel you're not quite the person you thought you were.

54

Those different worlds are something you can bring to your love life. This is a world that you can conjure up. This is a world your lover wants to be in. wants to be in with you. Wants to be in the kind of world you bring to your relationship. There you are. The two of you. It works.

Question 5

Do you have a sexual relationship at this time? If so, could you provide some details? You're married, longstanding relationship, new relationship, etc. If you do not have a sexual relationship at this time, do you want one?

OTHER PEOPLE'S ANSWERS

1.   I have to admit the only man I ever slept with was my husband. He's been dead for seven years now. I don't think I'm going to sleep with anyone else at this point in my life. Maybe. I'd like to. My husband always seemed to just want to get it over with. I would have liked a bit more.
Female, 60s.

2.   I have been divorced twice. I couldn't afford to get married again, which isn't very likely now I'm 66. I don't think I want to pay for it, but I've only had a couple of blowjobs. My wives never did it. I could handle some more.
Male, 60s.

3.   I'm married. Have been for a long time. We don't do it much. Only when he's drunk. Since I'm only telling this to myself, I had sex a fair amount before I got married and some of that was very good.
Female, 50s.

4.   As a married man of more than thirty years now I have to admit the sex part isn't very frequent. I don't think she cares at all.
Male, 50s.

5.   I have three men I see regularly. As gay men we are past that period of hanging out in bars, and that whole bar scene is kind of cheesy now anyway. I tried online. Not very good. I have different kinds of sex with these men. For the time being it's okay.
Male, 40s.

6.   I am among those who do not have a sexual relationship at this time. I know some other lesbians who have gone online and met women they enjoyed meeting. Yes, I definitely would like to be in love with someone.
Female, 40s.

7.   My situation is strange. I am involved with another trans

---

woman. We met on a computer site. We both used to be in men's bodies. Are we lesbians now? I don't know. Something between us has clicked. She's a wonderful person.
Female, 40s.

8.   I don't have a sexual relationship at this time which doesn't mean I don't have a sex life. I have a busy sex life with both men and women. I like having sex a lot and the people I have had as sex partners stay in touch. Too much.
Male, 40s.

9.   No sex in my life right now. None and that's okay with me. I don't like laying there under someone who is having a great time when I'm not. Not many men seem to be very aware of how the owner of the vagina is doing.
Female, 30s.

10.   I am engaged and will be married in two more months. Yes, we have a quite frequent sexual relationship and have for more than two years. I don't think either of us is interested in being with someone else. We are going to work at not getting bored with each other.
Male, 30s.

Your answer to Question 5: Do you have a sexual relationship at this time? If so, could you provide some details? If you do not, do you want one?

Monday, October 14, 2019

I didn't go to lunch today. A very good long-ago friend died last week. He was some six months older than I am and had been a fraternity brother in college with me. Theta Xi fraternity. He was from Long Island, New York, as were a number of my fraternity brothers, all of whom were much involved with sailing and boating.

The night before his funeral I was awaking all night long, running the lyrics of a World War II song through my head. "Please Give Me Something To Remember You By." About halfway through the night I realized this had something to do with my friend's death. I think the "something" he was giving me was the reiteration of that song as his burial approached the following morning.

His son has also become a very good friend, working in the advertising business as I did. In our conversation immediately after his father's death he said he had never forgotten my telling him what a friend of mine had said to me at one time as the years passed. My friend Norma. We had both been trained as dancers. I helped her get a start as an advertising copywriter. In a conversation she said to me, "We have been through some terrible times but we always looked good and we were always fun to be with." He told me that it was something he thought of frequently.

Thinking about moving in a social world that keeps us energized and responsible and amused, these are good words to remember. I don't want to be thought of as a lecturer, but "looking good" is a lot of work. But keeping yourself in good shape is great for your physical and mental health and makes you more competitive among your peers. As for, "being fun to be with," you yourself only need to think of those you know who qualify in that category and consider your own feelings towards them. Of course you want to see them and be with them. You see?

Diary Comment Eleven

"We are always fun to be with." This part of the quote from the previous diary entry prompts me to think of the two aspects of this quote that strongly affect your private life.

Firstly, the opposite of being fun to be with. I think it's a good idea to not overly confide our problems to our friends and acquaintances. I am not sure that discussing your difficulties does very much to relieve those difficulties. They will eventually be overcome and replaced with other similar life circumstances. People who know you are not going to look forward to meeting with you or having phone conversations if they are mostly recounting all the bad things that are going on in your life. You will find your contacts less frequent and your phone talks dwindling.

Perhaps it's better to give the impression that you don't have problems that you can't deal with by yourself. Now, that is attractive. That heads us into being fun to be with. Trying times can also be ridiculous. Which means you can talk about them to some degree while you laugh about them. For other people this is heartening as they are probably mulling over their own problems. Laughing with you helps them hoist up their own worries and proceed in a merrier way.

Also, if you're in a relationship, a jolly evening spent with friends interspersed with jokes and laughter and high spirits can continue on when you get home and into bedtime. Fooling around can easily become sexual.

IF you're not living together, the same high spirits can easily lead to going to somebody's home and fooling around there. It's not heaving breathing, heavy-going sex but another kind. I'll do this to you and you do this to me and light-heartedness pervades throughout.

You don't want someone to have sex with you because they feel sorry for you. That has hints of Clara Barton and Red Cross. If they are enjoying life because they have been with you, that's a different story.

Wednesday, October 16, 2019

Today started as every Wednesday does with yoga class. Yoga is very interesting if you have been exercising most of your life. With no weight-lifting but a lot of body stretching to prepare you for extreme meditation positions, your body becomes stronger and stronger. At least from talking with friends attending other classes at other yoga centers.

When I came home I reposed myself on my bed for a while to recover from all those stretches and one of my ancestors came into my mind as I semi-dozed there. I think she was my grandfather Sumner's grandmother. Her father had been a veteran of the Revolutionary War. Her name was Betsey Hadley Sumner Brockway Clough. She had been married three times. Her Sumner and Brockway children were much involved with each other. When my grandfather George Sumner married at 17 to a bride of 15 he then traveled to the Upper Peninsula of Michigan to work in the Brockway company store at Copper Harbor.

The copper mines were located on the northernmost edge of the thumb of land that extends into Lake Superior. A number of mines were there, each with a thriving town above each mine. The rest of Michigan, both upper and lower peninsulas, was still in the very early stages of being occupied. This strip of the state in the far north was much ahead of the rest of the state because of the valued copper.

The mines could only be reached by boat and were completely cut off in winter when the lakes were clogged with ice. While George Sumner and his very young wife, Clara Gee Sumner, were making their way to the north his grandmother Betsy was living on a farm outside Montague, the very rural town where I grew up. At some advanced age, perhaps in her sixties, she married a Mr. Clough and moved to the nearby and much larger city of Muskegon. How she met him and what prompted the marriage we don't know but certainly sex was part of it.

Her son shortly thereafter went to Muskegon and fetched his mother home again, telling her that she had been married enough times already. My mother told me this family history, which must have been recounted regularly as all of this happened well before my mother was born.

My last thought of the day. When you fly and see the age of the flight attendants you have to realize that more and more mature people are invading what was once an activity for young people only. When I see some attendants I realize that if there is a problem I will have to help them.

Diary Comment Twelve

I bring up my ancestor Betsy Hadley Sumner Brockway Clough from this diary entry. Here is someone who was the daughter of a Revolutionary War soldier. She kept getting married. Mixing her descendants in their occupations. And finally having one of them decide her last fling at marriage just wasn't suitable. Who knows? Mr. Clough may have been quite young, good looking, but drank too much. Betsy would have probably been able to figure out a way to stick it out with Mr. Clough in contemporary circumstances.

Which just brings us around to our subject. Betsy obviously still wanted a sexual relationship and was pursuing it throughout her life. Our Puritanical point of view that it's something to put aside as we grow older didn't apply to everyone even way back then. It certainly doesn't apply today.

Question 6

Do you know any sexually irregular persons? Gay, lesbian, trans, LGBT in any way? What is your takeaway?

OTHER PEOPLE'S ANSWERS

1.   My hairdresser is gay, as are all the rest of the hairdressers at the salon where I go. I am very used to being around them as I have gone there for quite a few years. I see a few people around that I think are homosexual but I don't talk to them about it.
Female, 60s.

2.   I had a friend in high school that I'm sure was gay, but we didn't know much about that stuff in Iowa where I grew up. Since then in the legal field the men seem to want to keep that information to themselves. The lesbians don't seem to find it a problem to let you know.
Male, 60s.

3.   One of my brothers is gay, the youngest one. Someone asked me when he came out and I told them I don't think he was ever in. He has had several long term relationships but is by himself now. He seems fine. We see each other a lot since we both still live in Cincinnati. He's always been very much there for me and I love him.
Female, 50s.

4.   Several of my fraternity brothers have decided they like men now after being married and having children. They have partners but I usually see them at lunch by themselves. We talk about the past. I don't think it's good for people to be pretending they are someone they are not. I don't feel any difference about them. We know each other very well.
Male, 50s.

5.   As a gay man I know quite a few other gay men. I also know a lot of people who aren't gay. I don't know transsexuals although I saw a young man put together as a young woman the other day. Very little make-up, good haircut, very nice low-key outfit. It didn't quite work. Too big a jaw.
Male, 40s.

6.   I'm a nurse so I spend my day with all kinds of people from all over. We are concerned with what's wrong with them, not their

sexuality. I know a lot of straight women from school and my being a lesbian doesn't come up. If you're not sick you're okay in the world I live in.
Female, 40s.

7.   I'm one of the people other people think about. When you become a trans person your family sees you in a dress and I've found does not seem to care. I work out of my home and I'm not meeting a lot of new people. I think most people are so loaded down with their own problems they don't pay a lot of attention.
Female, 40s.

8.   Sometimes when you're going to have sex with someone in a dress there's a surprise when you get down there. For me, once the dress is off it doesn't make any difference. I will say that the "irregulars" have had a lot more sex and know what they're doing. I should add, they also want to make sure that their partner is having good sex with them.
Male, 40s.

9.   I work in a busy office where lots of sales people come and go so you see lots of gay people, men and women. I haven't really seen any trans people but maybe they're good enough that I just don't get it. It's not something people pay a lot of attention to in the world I live and work in. Your sex is your business. How well you're doing your job is what they pay attention to.
Female, 30s.

10.   I don't have any gay friends but I see gay people around a lot and I'm glad they aren't getting any flak about it. I did see one trans person a few weeks ago. Now an airline stewardess and you would never guess. Kind of small, great hair, small features. Somebody who has crossed the line and nobody will know. The airline probably does. Good for them.
Male, 30s.

Your answer to Question 6: Do you know any sexually irregular persons? Gay, lesbian, trans, LGBT, in any way? What is your takeaway?

Thursday, October 17, 2019

I spoke to a friend in France today. It was early afternoon here in Miami Beach. Not as hot as it was yesterday when it was really boiling at midday. In France the leaves were falling, rainstorms were pouring down and it was early evening. It is at times like this that I deeply relish my life here in South Florida. I never feel the weather is too hot.

As you read this I want you to ask yourself if there is anywhere you would have liked to live that you haven't. Yet. I had never planned to or wanted to live in the Loire Valley, France. Until I went through on a chateaux tour. Long before France was a unified country, long before Paris was the largest and most central city, the Loire Valley and its chateaux existed. Each chateau the central dwelling of a titled Lord whose lands were leased out to the families who farmed it. They paid every year from the sale of crops for the right to have land. His was the title, as well as the judgment as to the beauty of the architecture of his chateau, the design of the furniture within, the sculptures and paintings that decorated it.

In other countries artists like Leonardo de Vinci, Michelangelo, all the great names, were employed by the landholders. Those who had the titles and stood behind someone they had selected to be the king of their territory. When you live in a countryside with this kind of history, you come to truly understand the country. Particularly someplace like the Loire Valley that stands virtually unchanged since the chateaux were first built centuries ago. Much later Paris became the capital of a country pulled together from a great variety of regions.

You don't have to learn the language of some place you'd like to live. You don't have to buy property. It doesn't even have to be a foreign country. You can come to Miami Beach in the summer when many inhabitants have gone north. The rents are very minimal. The people who remain are international, young, good-looking, very minimally dressed. You'll love it. Go somewhere no one goes. I have a home in Montevideo, Uruguay. No one goes there.

A large beautiful city on the Platte River is Montevideo. Small and wedged like a slice of pie in between Argentina and Brazil. Property prices are something like the 1930s in the United States. You can't buy a garage in Miami Beach for what I paid for a very large stone house built in the 1890s. One bathroom. No heat. A fabulous central courtyard some three stories high with a roll-off glass roof. Roll it away and you see the treetops waving above. Great. I love to renovate, so this was the dream project.

Many places you don't know you'd like to live there until you pass through. Not England. It never stops raining there. But Naples. South of Rome. Fantastic museums and no tourists. I visited a giant museum filled with masterpieces and shared it with two visiting Japanese persons.

Yes, it's a little dangerous but that adds some edge to your life experiences. People go there to trans-ship to the island of Capri. Everyone on Capri is from New York City and London and Paris. Naples is far more interesting.

You might try a little trip to Hong Kong. Not right now but when it settles down. A dizzying city built mostly on a vertiginous island just off the China coast. When you are there the city mounts to some seven levels. It is jammed with stores and people from all over the world. And from there a quick visit to China proper is just across the bay. A few hours away. Quick trains spirit you to Chinese cities. You can whirl up the coast to Shanghai, still the amazing place it was when all the international diplomats were there. So charged with people there was only a narrow lane for auto traffic in the center of the street when I was there. The sidewalks and main streets filled shoulder to shoulder with people. Like nothing you would ever see outside China.

It's true, it's a lot of work to actually do what you may have imagined to do in the past. But once fulfilled, you have a sense of having truly lived that there is no other way to have.

Diary Comment Thirteen

In this part of my diary I talk about finding who you truly are by visiting places very different from what you are used to. And also very different one from another.

It makes me think that you also have to visit different parts of yourself to find out who you truly are. Our culture is constantly telling us who we should be like. Each other for the most part. The range of possibilities that are acceptable to everyone is fairly narrow.

Yet when I think how much has changed in the world around me in my ninety years of residence in it, I am offered a lot of hope. Hope that more and more people will be able to have the life that they truly wish to have. We have had a black president. Something that would have been a wild fantasy through the early part of my life. We have same-sex relationships firmed up through marriage. Most people are not particularly unnerved if they know, work with, or socialize with someone whose partner is the same sex.

People change their sex. They have spent their lives wanting to wear the opposite sex's clothes. Now late in life your grandfather becomes your grandmother. Nobody cares very much.

Professor Kinsey discovered almost half a century ago that people have a wide range of sexual attraction in their personalities. There are those only attracted to the opposite sex. Those only attracted to the same sex. In between people range from being a little attracted to the same sex to being very attracted. In the center are those who are equally attracted to both sexes. Now those discoveries are widely recognized. Young men and women move back and forth finding out who they are most strongly attracted to. It may make their parents uneasy but there isn't a lot of them being dismissed from their families. The idea that you have chosen to be different only exists among the extremely conservative groups that still remain here. In this our country tends to be more conservative than the great part of the rest of the world.

All this is to let you know that your sex life may be in areas you haven't considered. Have resisted thinking about. If you are among the more mature citizens don't think that someone younger, someone of the same sex, someone of a different race may be drawn to you. Maybe finding your life experience, your self-confidence, your knowledge of the world around you makes them want to know you better.

These are the foreign countries of emotional life. You are a foreign country for someone else to experience. Go for it.

Saturday, October 19, 2019

Winter approaches up north. When I speak to friends in New York they report that the people in the streets are bundling up more and more. Here we remain in our shorts and T-shirts. It is breezier and sunny, floating brief rainstorms are overhead frequently but this is still the tropics.

My friend in Berlin reports that the leaves are changing and quite beautiful. That would never be enough reason for me to be willing to rush about muffled in an overcoat. I was brought up in Michigan. I saw plenty of falling leaves and raked them up, too. As a teenager I earned the money with which I went to college working as a gardener and groundskeeper for a wealthy retired lady in Montague, Michigan. Her name was Mrs. A. Merica. If you used that in a book people would think you were overdoing it. I can remember seeing it on her mailbox and thinking it was a little excessive even then. Her first name was Alice and who Mr. Merica was no one seemed to know or ever have seen him.

Just in the past few days I have started collecting quotes to reinforce my thinking about the enhancement of the later part of our lives. The famous dancer Alicia Alonso died last week. She was 98. She had terrible eyesight as quite a young dancer but she was remarkable even so. She was a great star when a prima ballerina had to also be a strong actress in roles like "Giselle." There she transitioned from a country girl to a ghost-like wraith. I saw her a good many times and she was a powerful presence on the stage. She was Cuban and retired there with a lot of help from President Fidel Castro. She was quoted as saying in her last years, "You don't have to think about how old you are. You have to think about how many things you want to do and how to do them and keep on going." She added, "I think I am going to be 200 years old. So I hope all of you do have the same fortune. I would hate to be alone." I loved reading this. She really was a trouper.

I also read an interview with Maye Musk, the very striking white-haired mother of Elon Musk. She is the person that evidently set the stride for that young financier businessman. She at 71 is still very attractive but was quoted as saying, "I think it's better to be interesting than to be beautiful." Yes, Mrs. Musk. Yes.

Now I must think about preparing to see a new musical up in

Fort Lauderdale this evening. A new show that has already had a run in New York called "Daddy Issues." My friend David Goldyn wrote it and is one of the leads. I've worked in a number of his mini-musicals and look forward to seeing it. He also directed it and is very good to work with. Frequently you have to do what the director wants in rehearsals and then let yourself go once you are on stage. Not with Mr. Goldyn. He gets the best out of his cast.

Diary Comment Fourteen

This October diary entry is largely about people growing older and still experimenting with their lives. Continuing to explore who they are and what is going on around them.

I have been wanting to write something about S&M since it plays a large role in a good many people's sex lives. That's Sado-Masochism. Which is to either threaten your sex partner in a very punishing way, or to be the person receiving the punishment.

This morning discussing this planned comment with a friend he disclosed that he had once had a male partner who wanted to be hit in the face while they were having sex until he had his orgasm. I said, "One of my rules is to never do anything that damages your appearance." He replied, "It wasn't my appearance that was getting damaged."

Perhaps you have had some of the experiences I have had. I have had a sex partner who wanted to strangle me with my bathrobe waist tie. Wrapping it around my neck and pulling on it he would ask, "How is that?" I would look back at him and say, "You know this doesn't interest me at all." The fact that I didn't struggle and scream undercut all his interest in these kinds of activities. It gave me an insight as to what some people find exciting mixed in with their sexual activities, however.

Another person with whom I was involved for a very long period of time at one point had developed an interest in being urinated on. If you went to the bathroom he would follow you to see if there was some possibility of that.

I thought of this as being linked in some way to poor self-esteem. I never wanted to be a party to reinforcing anyone's poor self-esteem, although I would guess there are any number of others who would think it a novelty and be glad to oblige him. It would also mean you would have to clean up the bathroom after, which I did not want to do.

He moved on from this period of his life although I don't think he ever raised his self-esteem in any major way. Even though he was a very handsome man with a great body.

I knew another man who was very heavily tattooed only where his brief underpants covered. With no clothing his tattoos almost looked like some kind of undergarment. I would not know where to place this longing to have a tattoo but not wanting others to think poorly of you if they might disapprove of tattoos? I have no idea and this was the only time I ever saw that phenomenon.

My own thought is that Sado-Masochism is linked to sexuality at the level of low self-esteem; punishing others or being punished yourself for the act of sex. However I would never announce that I am sure of this. There are many facets of the human personality. If it gives people pleasure to manifest them and they are not damaging another person's life then it is none of my business.

Question 7

If you are in a relationship would you consider having sex outside the relationship with a third person? What if your partner did? How about both of you with a third person, man or woman?

OTHER PEOPLE'S ANSWERS

1.   I never had sex with anyone else except my husband but now as I look back it's because it just never came up. When we had been married quite a while if some man had wanted to have an affair I might have. Maybe my husband did and I just never thought about it. Part of that is I didn't work. He did. He met a lot more people.
Female, 60s.

2.   Now it doesn't matter but my second wife was my secretary and we had sex a lot before I got a divorce and married her. Afterwards she kept a strict eye on me. She knew what could happen.
Male, 60s.

3.   I almost had an affair with our plumber. He came to the house a lot during a renovation and we got to know each other. I used to wonder what it would be like to have sex with him. I could tell he was interested. He was married, too. I didn't and since I'm still married to the same man I think I did the right thing. I think I did.
Female, 50s.

4.   I was in the army for two years before I met my wife. It was that or you were drafted. I served in Vietnam but not for very long. I slept with the whores just like everybody else. Maybe more than everybody else. I got the clap twice. After that I didn't fool around. I sure didn't want to give my wife a venereal disease.
Male, 50s.

5.   When I have been in a relationship I have done threesomes. I never cheated on my lover and didn't let him know. I counted on him to do the same thing. The thing I don't like about threesomes is that it usually ends up with one person watching and that was usually me.
Male, 40s.

6.   When people start messing around outside their relationship

it is because they're bored. They probably own a house or something with their partner so fool around a little on the side. I've only seen this. I wouldn't do this.
Female, 40s.

7.   Maybe when there are more trans women and men around they'll get into a relationship and then fool around. Now it's so difficult you're not going to do something to screw it up.
Female, 40s.

8.   How about orgies? I've been in plenty of those and what you find out is that lots of people love to watch. More than to have sex. Kind of like theater. Far from romance.
Male, 40s.

9.   I'm very big on love. I don't really want to sleep with someone unless we have the emotional thing going on and if we don't I don't want to have sex. So the third partner possibility hasn't come up in my life. Who knows what might happen in the future but I don't think so.
Female, 30s.

10.   Definitely not. I'm about to get married. We are going to make this work.
Male, 30s.

Your answer to Question 7: If you are in a relationship would you consider having sex outside the relationship with a third person? What if your partner did? How about both of you with a third person?

Monday, October 21, 2019

I stayed up late on Saturday night at the theater and then yesterday went to my strenuous yoga class in the morning. I am just regaining my brains today to report back. The show "Daddy Issues" was amusing in that the plot has a young gay man lie to his goading parents and tell them he is in fact the father of a ten year old boy. His college sweetheart became pregnant a decade earlier. He had never married her but knew his son existed, all of this being complete fiction. His parents demand to see their grandson and he enlists a young boy who lives in his building to play the role. There are several alternatives to who will play the boy's mother. One of them is a very tall drag queen who appears excessively put together for anyone's mother. The audience liked this a lot. The plot resolves itself with the mother of the young boy who plays the role of his son appearing. She is in fact the college sweetheart and the boy is in fact his son. This pleased everyone very much.

The play was very well directed by my friend David Goldyn, who wrote the show and plays the father of the gay young man. I was mostly impressed with the ten-year-old who played the son. He was quite a remarkable little actor. He was a ten-year-old playing a ten-year-old. Please, remember yourself at 10. Could you have been onstage for the better part of a more than two-hour play and stayed right up there in your role with all the reactions and observations when the focus wasn't on yourself? He was pretty amazing and should be going on to major things. I hope he has the right parents.

Last night I was reading the new issue of GQ magazine and came across an article about men meeting with each other and letting go in the group about things that really bothered them. Things about themselves. Things that weren't particularly masculine. The author of the article writes at one point: "Sometimes I forget that my body is as much 'me' as my brain is. Sometimes I behave like my body is a fleshy robot, the sole purpose of which is to carry my very important brain around. But the renowned PTSD specialist and author of 'The Body Keeps the Score' Bessel van der Kolk, M.D. told me, 'We have a brain in order to make sure our body is okay. Our body is not an appendage of our brain. We are our bodies.'"

This is the sort of lecture I am never going to give other people but I was surprised to find it in a popular magazine. In this country we are in many ways taught to think that the things our bodies want to do are wrong and will get us into trouble. I think a lot of the stress that bothers people is because they are either ignoring what their bodies need or feeling guilty because of it. My feeling is that you have to pay attention to what your body wants you to do. It is your body. If it is damaging to someone else's life, obviously you can't do it. But if it isn't, like watching porn for instance, please, be my guest. You can be kind to yourself as well as other people.

Diary Comment Fifteen

Reading this diary entry I was much reminded of the very talented child actor I mention. I had just read this morning in the *New York Times* an obituary of a professor who had started his career as a child Quiz Kid during World War II. It was a very popular radio show in a time when many adult male actors were in military service. Only nine years old when he started, he was brilliant answering any kind of mathematic or scientific question. This was done under the supervision of a very commanding mother.

Later he regretted it, as other children his age did not like him and as he proceeded with his studies he found himself insulted and derided by his fellow students.

Child actors also have some family member supervising their careers. In many ways they have to forfeit their childhoods. On the other hand perhaps they are having an extended adulthood in this manner.

I recount all this as I had a sex life that began very early. Another boy a year older than myself began to want to be with me all the time when I was four. He was five. We had something that approached sex by taking off our clothes and laying down on top of each other. He had found some small pornographic booklets having to do with Popeye the Sailor doing bad things with Olive Oyl and other cartoon characters. In this way we learned what adults did. He told others that when we grew up he was going to marry me.

As I have written before I never felt guilty about my gayness and though I continued to have sexual encounters with this boy until he graduated from high school a year ahead of me, I never thought of him in a romantic way. It was just something we both wanted to do and we did it. He enlisted in the Navy as I remember and later married a young woman from a neighboring town. He had a family and died a number of years ago in his early 70s.

In later stages of my life I have found men drawn to me who were clearly considered heterosexual. Why this is so I have never determined. Again, all sexuality seems to be far from clear cut.

—

Tuesday, October 22, 2019

The *New York Times* Sunday edition had a big special section on health, which I just read today. The part of it that interested me most was on sleep. It went on at great length about how famous people and wealthy people often only sleep some four hours a night because their lives require a great deal more time handling things than the average person.

It goes on to explain that this is not good and can be harmful health-wise, and the rest of the article is devoted to explanations on how to prepare for sleep so as to be able to have a longer sleep pattern.

I had no idea that many people get up at five o'clock in the morning and do their meditating or exercise or other activities before they start the day. It sounds horrible to me and it also suggests that these people live alone. I don't think I could share my life with one of those five-o'clockers since I sleep some 12 hours a night. I get up at 9:30 A.M. because my big dog Baby somehow can tell time and demands I get up. Not to make poo-poo but because she wants to go out and romp with other dogs and go kiss-kiss with children being pushed around by their parents. Everyone knows her and she is known as the happiest dog in the neighborhood.

I love to sleep. I always did. When I was working a very heavy schedule in New York in advertising I never got up before noon on Saturday and Sunday. Just a few days ago I was chatting with a young woman as we were waiting to go into our yoga class. Somehow sleep came up as a subject and when I told her that I usually slept twelve hours a night she told me that she did the same thing. I was so pleased to hear it as I suspect that most people would disapprove of spending half of your time asleep. Here was someone else that packed all their living into half the day. It made me wonder how many other people were passing in and out of my life with long sleep patterns. A lot I hope.

As I get older I find I sleep even more of the time and it doesn't make me feel uneasy about aging. I remember being told once that the 1930s film star Dolores Del Rio in her retirement slept almost all the time. It certainly makes life easier for those around you. "Where is she/he?" "They're in bed sleeping."

Just to add one more thing as we have sleep as a topic. One

—

thing I strongly advise all my friends is to ignore thinking about their lives when they wake in the night. I am sure that not all of our brain is fully awake and that the results are our thoughts are very negative thoughts and we think about what a mess our lives are and what are we going to do about it? It is equally true when we first wake up. Our minds contemplate everything that is wrong with our lives. The positive upper layer of thought has not yet to join us.

I wait until I am halfway through walking the dogs before I allow myself to consider what is going on in my life. Then immediately the new projects and what may occur in the near future pop up. You think of the person you forgot to call in Hollywood. You remember the meeting you are having on Friday. Lots of things look promising. You find yourself looking forward to all kinds of things that never came up in the night or at dawn. I promise you this is true. A bit of hope that I am holding out for you.

Diary Comment Sixteen

As I have been making Diary Comments I have been depending more and more on my subconscious releasing memories to me. I have come to think that we really never forget anything. It is just as the years accumulate there are more and more memories. All of them are tucked away in the subconscious. Many of them, usually the most recent, slip away from us. But if we question our subconscious it will return them to us.

In this entry, which is primarily about the large presence of sleep in my life, my subconscious has returned a memory to me that has nothing to do with sleep at all but has a pertinent light to throw upon this book's subject.

At one point in my life I was on a travel venture with a group of friends and acquaintances. Nearing our return we were all in a hotel together, perhaps somewhere in the Caribbean, in the room next to mine was someone I had had a long relationship with some years before, now terminated for some time. There was a door between our rooms which I had ignored.

Shortly before dinner one evening I returned to my room and passed the interior door as I entered. For some reason I turned the knob and it opened. I entered and heard the shower running. I took off my clothes and went to the shower and entered. No words were spoken but it was clear that my former romance had thought something like this might happen. Sex followed.

Returning to my room to change my clothes for dinner, the two of us then went to the dining room and entered together. As we approached the table I noticed some of our travel partners taking notice and I sensed that they were considering why the two of us might be coming to dinner a bit late. We took our separate seats at the table and the meal progressed.

These kinds of happenings occur in our lives. I think it is better that they do than that they do not. We shall see what my subconscious retrieves from my past as this book approaches its conclusion.

Question 8

Does masturbation play any kind of major role in your life? Has it ever?

OTHER PEOPLE'S ANSWERS

1.　　My husband used to like having me do it to him but he didn't want to do it to me. Or anything much like it.
Female, 60s.

2.　　All teenage boys do it a lot and so did I. Now I'm single. I wake up in the night and do it once in a while. Not a lot.
Male, 60s.

3.　　I used to do it quite a lot when I was a young woman before I was married. Once I did it with the handle of a hairbrush. Does that count?
Female, 50s.

4.　　Maybe this is my secret sex thing. I always masturbated a lot and I still do a couple of times a week if I've been reading something sexy or see something sexy. I get erections very easily.
Male, 50s.

5.　　When you're gay you probably masturbate more than other men do usually when they get middle-aged. You see guys and you get interested and then nothing doing. So you masturbate.
Male, 40s.

6.　　I have an electronic masturbation instrument. Is that the right word? I don't like going around feeling needy. If I feel like it, I'll do it.
Female, 40s.

7.　　Yes, of course. As a trans woman I have a number of penis-shaped objects I use to relieve myself of tension. Sometimes with another trans person, I let them use them on me.
Female, 40s.

8.　　I have sex with lots of different people and often with the men it winds up with masturbation because that's what they like best. Women less. They need the whole person more I guess. I should write a book about this.
Male, 40s.

9.　　I don't ever talk about this but I masturbate about once a

week mainly so I don't spend too much time thinking about sex.
Female, 30s.

10.   Before I was involved with my fiancée if I wasn't seeing some woman with whom I had sex I always masturbated quite often. In the shower. Three or four times a week?
Male, 30s.

Your answer to Question 8: Does masturbation play any kind of major role in your life? Has it ever?

Wednesday, October 23, 2019

Yoga class in the morning today. My friend Reniel Diaz is attending nowadays and we had lunch afterwards. He has a new project of decorating a home for wealthy relatives and I brought him pages I had on file or had recently pulled from contemporary magazines reflecting the new interiors that do not have art on their very expensive white walls. It's very interesting as to how decorators manage to place plants and sculpture on the floor near the ends of very long and expansive couches to give the room some feeling of welcome and prestige.

Among the photos were some of bedrooms, which followed the decorative plan with no decoration on the walls but overly long headboards, large potted plants along the wall base, decorated door frames: all to give a kind of longitudinal luxury to the room.

Looking at these made me think about bedrooms and how one furnishes rooms when you're living with someone you love who doesn't or can't sleep in the same bed with you. There are a number of reason for this. My sister's husband snored so loudly no one could sleep within about two or three rooms from him. I mean really loud. When they visited me he slept in a bedroom below mine and he shook the walls.

There are also people who just can't fall asleep with another person in the bed. So they must sleep separately. I tell you all this, having a lover of my own at the moment with this condition, to give you advice. Make sure that wherever you live, home or apartment, that one of you sleeps in a double bed even if you are there alone. If you can both sleep in double beds that is the best of all solutions.

If you both sleep in single beds that lessens the probability of romance suddenly overtaking you and falling into each other's arms and into bed. I myself don't mind if I sleep alone at night if at dawn I can wander to the other's room and fall into bed with them. They can complain about my waking them up. I don't mind that.

So there's my advice. Don't have a home without at least one double bed. Of course your guest room should have a double bed also if you have such a room. But you already know that.

Diary Comment Seventeen

This diary entry is all about sleeping and I have discussed sleeping a good bit in the book. So I will not add any further information at this point.

I can mention that I very recently read about an unmarried couple who lived in one apartment and she kept a separate one where she went to work every day. A busy writer, she maintains a life apart at this separate home for herself. I am assuming that he from time to time drops by her homestead and she undoubtedly has a bedroom with a double bed.

Of course in a Pandemic they would have to share one dwelling to keep their relationship from falling apart. But perhaps not. Interesting.

As I proceed through this book I can see that for relationships to continue both parties have to continue growing and changing and fulfilling themselves. In this way they can hold the other party's attention and interest.

Coming to know someone completely and thoroughly in their early twenties, when most relationships begin, is not to say you will still know that person well in their forties. Or their sixties, or further. In any sexual relationship the start-off has certain to do with physicality. As the relationship progresses it becomes a combination of the physical and the partner's personhood.

When people contact me from the past I can tell they are relating to a personality they knew from those now quite distant years. I respond by playing back that personality but there is more there. And perhaps less of that person they once knew. Evolving as we all are quite capable of doing tells us that we can continue to be interesting…even fascinating…at whatever age we find ourselves.

—

Monday, October 28, 2019

A much younger friend (actually the son of a good friend) emailed me recently to tell me about his beginning to go to a meditation center. He wrote, "The world looks funnier than it used to." I like that reaction. I have meditated daily for many years now. Over fifty. It can be tough when you really get into it. That's the main reason I don't recommend it. My point of view is that if people know me they will perhaps connect the fact I don't complain a lot with my meditation practice. I'm not going to hustle about urging anyone to do anything.

In fact I do tell people who smoke and drink too much that it's tough on their looks. People don't give a hoot about their health but immediately react if they think it affects the way they look. It does. Lots of wrinkles.

To get back to meditation and the world beginning to look like a funny place. Meditation does give you a broader view of your own life. You come to view it as though it was someone else's. You come to see that a lot of things that perhaps frightened you a little were not frightening.

My great friend Jean Ann Zuver said, "Only silly people act serious. Serious people act silly." Which is really to say that as you mature you see that many of the people you are interacting with are not to be taken seriously. Barely competent, they surround themselves with a world where everything seems very important. But as the Bessie Smith song says, "You put a smile on your face and keep your big mouth shut."

I tell you all this because interacting with the world and seeing how silly much of it is results in a self-confident person. Self-confidence makes you attractive to a lot of people. Particularly to younger people. And as you grow more mature and sophisticated with the passing years you need to spend more time with those a good bit younger than yourself.

Your peers who have not come to view the world as you do withdraw more and more from a world where people look good and are fun to be with. You have to skid down several decades, maybe more, to spend your time with those who view the world as you do. Or who want to learn from you how to view the world as a place that is not so much threatening as amusing.

—

In one of my cabaret shows when I came onstage I said, "There are only three reasons to know someone. They are beautiful, they are interesting, they are good. If you're not beautiful and you can't manage to be interesting I highly recommend that you be good." Later someone asked me, "But how about if that person can do something for you?" I told them, "You will owe them something in return and time spent with them will be largely boring. Do you really want someone like that in your life?"

Diary Comment Eighteen

You have just read a good bit about how being interesting and self-confident can be just as important sexually as being physically alluring. That's conjectured. Here's fact.

You can introduce a new interest of yours, or even one you've been with for some time, to pornography. You can buy books, you can buy photographs, you can watch movies, lots of them. You will be amazed at the amount of variety that there is in pornography. Every variant that people have ever dallied with has been made into a movie. You should do it just to get your partner or potential partner to give you some idea of what they might be interested in.

Most people have no idea what is possible among their fellowmen. You may very well learn a good bit yourself.

Another contribution from my subconscious today was to have you consider your posture if you are among the more mature and sophisticated of the readers of this book. As they get older many... I think we can say most... people begin to stoop. Women do this to conceal both their enlarging and slipping bosoms. Men because they are not moving around as much as they used to. Gravity is struggling with us and pulling us earthward, the top of our bodies first.

It's a dead giveaway to aging, so I am urging you to stand up. Really. Take a look at yourself sideways in the mirror. If you can stand to do it, stand there with the bulk of your clothes off. You will see that if you just make the effort to throw your shoulders back, pull in your stomach, and lift your chest that you are standing an inch or so taller than you were before.

It doesn't really require exercise. It just requires some concentration on your part. Particularly when sitting also. At the lunch table get your behind under you, push that chest up and shoulders back. Get your chin up, lift that spoon and dominate the conversation.

Good posture telegraphs self-confidence. Self-confidence is very appealing to others. Stand up and be popular!

Question 9

Would you consider a sexual relationship with someone much younger? Older? A difference racially? The same sex? Please explain at some length.

OTHER PEOPLE'S ANSWERS

1.   Are you kidding? If someone was interested in me sexually I would be available. Same sex maybe not. I know very little about that.
Female, 60s.

2.   I would certainly be interested in sex with a younger woman. I don't know if there are many older than me I would want to have sex with. Maybe. Depends on the woman. If she is black, Asian, Indian, again it only depends on the woman. Other men, definitely not.
Male, 60s.

3.   Men who are sort of in my age range are really the only ones I meet. If some man showed up who was really interested he could be younger or older and I would especially be interested in a man of a very different race. Black, yes, and also Asian or mixed race but a little bit less. Maybe if a woman really knew what she was doing I could give it a go.
Female, 50s.

4.   I find it hard to believe a younger woman would be interested in me if there is nothing in it for her financially but should that happen I would be interested. An older woman I don't think so. The younger woman can be of any race. Women are women and I love that about them. Men I don't think so. Maybe if he were young and very girly I might give it a try. Just to see what it's like.
Male, 50s.

5.   Younger or older women are not for me. I'm gay. Men in those categories will all interest me pretty much the same. I don't have any other races that I would turn down. There's always something down there in their pants.
Male, 40s.

6.   Where am I in this? I think I'm still a younger woman and I would always want to know an older woman better. Working at the hospital I have met lots of lesbians of different races and been with

---

some. Black women always interest me. There's a kind of power there.
Female, 40s.

7.   Trans is such a small category I would never be picky about anyone who was interested in me sexually. Every other person is an experience. Those who have fought to find themselves will always interest me a lot.
Female, 40s.

8.   I take every person one at a time. Whether it's a man or a woman, no matter the age or the race, if they ring my bell sexually I am willing to explore who they are and what they want to do.
Male, 40s.

9.   Older men always having something going for them for me. I guess being from the mid-west I don't really know how I'd react to someone from another race. But this is the 21st century. You can't automatically think no. But another woman? Not for me.
Female, 30s.

10.   I am about to be married to a woman to whom I plan to be loyal sexually the rest of my life. So I don't consider other possibilities.
Male, 30s.

Your answer to Question 9: Would you consider a sexual relationship with someone much younger? Much older? Different racially? The same sex? Explain at length.

Tuesday, October 29, 2019

I went to Spanish class last night at Miami-Dade College. It prompted me to write about meeting more people. New people. Younger people. People from all over the world.

If you want to inject some romance into your life you have to break out of your usual routine. Meet people you are not going to meet in your daily life. Put some demands upon yourself to commence doing things you haven't been doing before. Perhaps ever before.

Learning a new language is a great solution in many ways. It is usually quite available. It will certainly have a variety of people attending. And through those people you will be meeting even more new people. More possibilities for romance or sex or whatever it is that you have in mind.

I first started studying Spanish when I was in high school. Our teacher was a middle-aged lady named Mona Gerred who had been teaching Latin until that year. The Second World War was raging around the world and evidently educators had decided a second language should be more functional than Latin in daily life. Miss Gerred was just one lesson ahead of the class. I have no idea where she might have gotten information on pronunciation but we forged along. To little avail, I should add.

Through the years I have made other ventures in taking courses when something was available.

Most recently I was attending an evening course at a local high school primarily designed for Spanish speakers to learn English. There was one course for English speakers to learn Spanish. It was pretty fascinating as the only people in the class who were born in the United States were my friend Harry and myself. The others were either Russian, Hungarian, Ukrainian, you name it. They were all youngish people working for foreign countries who were discovering that many of their clients were Spanish speakers. To do their business more effectively they were learning Spanish.

The Russians were mostly young, good-looking women. What Russian businesses they worked for we never learned but they undoubtedly had many clients from Argentina, Ecuador, Chile and the other countries south of the border. Their English was always very good and they explained that learning Spanish from English was much easier than Spanish from Russian.

Unfortunately our teacher couldn't manage to teach classes that were useful to beginning students. The beginners dropped out rapidly and eventually the class had so few students the school cancelled it.

Harry and I have moved on to Miami-Dade although Harry was loathe to leave the Russian beauties behind. However, at Miami-Dade we found yet another world of people we would in no way have met otherwise.

In this class of 15 students we found ourselves surrounded by students from Thailand, Brazil, Sweden, Hungary, and a few Native Americans. All of them quite young and very energetic. We also found ourselves with a male teacher who had plenty of strength to get us through our three hour class. Which we would be taking twice a week.

He organized it well. We began by learning the past tense structure of the three different forms of Spanish verbs and then marched on to learn vocabulary for all the things one does around the house. Then finally chatting with each other about household duties we liked and didn't like.

My chat partners were a young Thailandese woman and a young Hungarian man. My Spanish was perhaps just a bit ahead of theirs so I could propose questions and they could dig around trying to speak answers.

There were perhaps three attractive young women in the class so Harry is looking forward to more of these interlocking personalities classes. As I said when starting today's thoughts, if you want to meet some new people with potential for your life, start studying Spanish, French, and Chinese. Whatever appeals to you most. You'll be off and running in a jiffy.

Diary Comment Nineteen

The diary of this date is concentrated upon studying another language as a tool to meeting new people, many of them young and energetic. That is certainly a good idea but this Diary Comment is going to leap forward and assume that you have now moved along and are in a relationship that needs to become much more sexual.

This can also apply to those of the readers who have been in a relationship for some time that may need a little energizing.

From my own life I can suggest that you start taking baths instead of showers. I began taking baths when I had a highly stressful advertising career. At the end of my day I would fill a tub, find something to read and clamber in for a 45-minute minimum stay. I felt I had to soak off the negative vibrations of the day. All the verbal harassment, unhappy atmosphere, and tension that surrounded trying to sell clients new ideas and new directions.

It worked. I could go to bed having shed the battering of the day and sleep well in preparation for another day of similar ambiance to the day before.

What I also learned was that if anyone else was around, they were drawn to your undressed body loitering in the bathtub. Should they come into the bathroom while you are entubbed you can chat with them. Even leaving the door ajar so as to be able to chat with them. This tends to draw them in. you are not shut behind a curtain with water pouring down over you. You are lounging in front of their eyes. With nothing on.

You can even reach up and touch them in inviting areas. Suppose you suggest they take off their clothes and join you in the tub? For some reason this seems to be a fairly common fantasy. They probably will. One more step towards enhancing your sex life.

If you are too embarrassed to do all this perhaps the non-embellishment of your sex life may be your fault. Think about this.

Friday, November 1, 2019

Last night was Halloween and I hosted a table of six at Panizza restaurant squarely on Lincoln Road to see the costumes go by. There were many and as we seated ourselves the tide was turning from parents with their children to more sophisticated arrivals. The children were painted up a good bit to look like television characters they know (I'm guessing) and some of the mothers were very scantily put together. I wonder what the children may remember with Mom toddling about in next to nothing.

This was not of great consequence in comparison with what many of the wilder ones were wearing. Or not wearing. Buttocks were very much in evidence. Many of the young women were put together as tiny-skirted brides or fluffy-skirted ballet dancers. This allowed them to leave the lower half of their buttocks fully and droopily exposed. This has been a big look this season in short-shorts. The back half being trimmed very high for maximum hang-out. I read in the paper that one young woman was so attired to go to dinner with her parents and her father appeared with his own shorts trimmed high to expose the bottom half of his buttocks. The daughter was very shocked and begged her father to please not appear in public that way. He pointed out that they were both attired exactly alike. I find this all very 21st century.

Many of the gay men were also wearing very flimsy see-through underpants as their lower-half garment. No matter what the rest of the costume displayed they were clearly showing off what they considered one of their most important attractions. (Is that "two" when you discuss buttocks?) A number of quite tall gay men were dressed as women in bright red frocks or suits, one with additional mauve high heels.

Among my guests was a friend who goes to Spanish class with me who just dropped by the table to join us for a drink. He brought along an acquaintance, a much-experienced actor now largely retired. I was the only one at the table who had no experience of living in San Diego, California. The others had lived there or been students there or both. They talked about San Diego in great detail. The only thing I could join them in was when they discussed people they had known in theater or modeling work. I had known some of these people also in my years in the advertising business.

—

One was a blonde model who had moved up from her modeling career to marry a rock star. I pointed out that she had slept with half the eastern seaboard as she rose in her career. It was well known that if you hired her you slept with her. At least that was her reputation.

I said, "Can you spell 'slut'?" My niece, who had been a model, said, "But she was a really nice person." And I was reminded once again that we were in the 21st century. If you have a reputation for sleeping around a lot it isn't much more meaningful than shaking hands a lot.

I should go on record that although I have worked in some milieus where sleeping with a great many different people was commonplace, it was never my lifestyle. Perhaps because I slept with a number of different people in my teen years, I was very romantic as an adult and didn't see sex as some sort of sport or activity. When I was involved with someone I did not also sleep with anyone else or everyone else as a sort of side thing many thought it was okay to do. As many of the people I knew did. This has always been my style. When I am in love with someone that is it. No fooling around. Which is probably why I survived the H.I.V. epidemic.

I lived through that period and went to see many dying men in the hospital. Most of the people I expected to still have as friends as life passed by were lost at that time. I can remember going to see them and being given plastic gloves and face mask to wear as I sat at their bedside. At that time almost nothing was known as to how the disease was communicated. I always refused to wear the facemask and gloves. I always felt that if I was there to cheer them up and communicate with them I wasn't going to hide behind a mask. It was a very sad period. Many people were dying at the same time. It was advised to not visit them for fear of becoming ill myself. I can remember going to large wards, rows of hospital beds, and I would be the only visitor. If you are thinking that I am asking for some credit for my bravery, I am.

At any rate, to continue. I think being promiscuous reduces the impact of a romantic relationship by a great deal. I think if you want a lot of sex you are best off having it with one other person. If you fear it will become boring, that is only a discredit to you and your lack of imagination as to what two people can do with one body each to work with.

I think this is a subject that should be thought about and dealt with more. In a conversation with a friend a few days ago he pointed out that a couple we both knew had recently gotten married after being together for some eight years. He said, "They probably haven't had sex for a couple of years now." It made me stop and think I have only had four major love affairs as an adult. My policy has always been that if my lover no longer wants to sleep with me, the relationship is over. Adios. I'm not interested in having a roommate.

I am always somewhat mystified about couples who are together because they get along well, are interested in the same things, etc. All of that has nothing to do with sex. I have already voiced my feelings that we have both our bodies and our minds to be concerned about. And if we neglect our bodies and their needs and requests and devote ourselves only to what our minds are concerned with, that may well be why we become ill.

To finish today's diary entry I will recount something sexy that happened in my life. I was living in a tiny, ancient apartment in Greenwich Village in New York City with my first major lover. We had a tiny bedroom with a single bed, a small living room with a kind of narrow daybed where I slept. That was the sleeping space.

I was being visited by a young former naval officer who had shared duties with me aboard the aircraft carrier where I first served when I was in the U.S. Navy. I had taken cushions off my daybed for him to sleep on in the center of the miniscule living room floor.

We had just had dinner with a female friend and he had offered to see her off to the subway before returning to our little apartment. In his brief absence my lover decided that he needed to make love. He was just achieving climax with me on the daybed when we heard the garden gate open. He managed to get across the room and into the bathroom just as our houseguest opened the apartment door. I pretended I was asleep. In such moments difficult embarrassments never appear, protected by a few seconds of timing. Since my lover was not very experimental in the department of sex I enjoyed seeing him whirled through a bit of drama.

Diary Comment Twenty

This diary entry is quite sexy so perhaps the comment about it need not be quite so sex loaded. It does make the point that it is certainly more meaningful and certainly safer to be developing your sexual fulfillment with the same person. For me, there has always been something about having a lot of sex with a lot of strangers that is kind of "dog-ish." That whole thing you see among pets of running up and smelling parts. And to give pets some credit, they are not particularly interested if the other pet is not in heat and ready to participate.

My counseling here is more about being sexy than having sex. It's about how you smell. Of course you bathe regularly or shower and use deodorant. But you should have a personal fragrance. I don't think women should have a wide variety of perfumes and colognes they use. And I think men should always have a men's cologne that they wear to add to their distinction and singularity.

Interestingly some fragrances will be enhanced by your wearing them and some will not. Your personal aura integrates with them so some smell much better on you than others. If you haven't really considered all this before, choose the fragrance you consider your personal and singular way to project yourself and ask others what they may think of it.

For myself I have a very low threshold of smelling so I don't really smell the fragrance of other people nor my own. However, I have worn Givenchy Gentleman for quite a few years. In fact since I worked as a TV director in France in the 1970s. In France of course no one would think of entering the outdoor world without their fragrance or cologne well applied. It's a must in that country.

Mixing with a great many people every day I chose Givenchy Gentleman and got playback that it smelled good on me. Some women even said, "You smell better than I do!" which confirmed for me I was wearing the right thing and I have never considered another.

All of this to say, get your smell and it will all be part of the urge others have to know you better and even go further than that.

Question 10

Sexually, are there some activities you have not had that you would like to know more about? Can you add info as to why you haven't experienced these sexual activities yet?

OTHER PEOPLE'S ANSWERS

1.   I have a fantasy of being in bed with a man who is much larger than I am. He could even be quite fat. Too big to get on top of me. So we do several things. Sideways. Me on the top. I think sex is about taking responsibility for another person. My husband never really wanted to.
Female, 60s.

2.   How about this? I have never had sex with two women at the same time. I think it's me in one and my mouth on the other. In her crotch. I guess I am never going to do this.
Male, 60s.

3.   In my head I have wondered about what it would be like at a big sex party. Having different men come up and have a little sex. Maybe a lot of sex. What would that be like?
Female, 50s.

4.   I know there are strap-on penises that lesbians use and I guess gay men. I wonder what it would be like to have a woman put on a strap-on penis and have sex with me like she was a man? A penis and breasts.
Male, 50s.

5.   Have I tried everything I never imagined doing? Only with other men of course. I can wonder what it would be like on horseback. Galloping across the plains, him behind me in the saddle. I'll bet cowboys have done this.
Male, 40s.

6.   I have this fantasy that I am on top with a penis. This isn't the same thing as having a penis strapped on you. That's like acting out a part in a play or something. Not the same.
Female, 40s.

7.   My biggest thing would be having sex with two men at the same time. It could still happen. I'm not that old. For a trans that would be a big experience.

Female, 40s.

8.　　Would falling in love with someone come under the heading of something you've never done? When I read about it or see it on a movie I realize I have never had those kinds of feelings for someone else. I can still hope that someone will fall in love with me and drag me into their love.

Male, 40s.

9.　　I have all kinds of fantasies of things to do with men. Sitting on top of them. Frontwards, backwards, in the front seat of the car. In a swing. In a hammock. On a huge lawn at night with a party going on in a big house nearby. All of these things could happen. I'd better get going.

Female, 30s.

10.　　I'm getting married. My wish was to fall in love and now I am in love. We don't do anything particularly wild in bed but it makes me feel very complete. I think the same thing is happening for the woman in my life.

Male, 30s.

Your answer to Question 10: Sexually, are there some activities you have not had that you would like to know more about? What? Why not?

Saturday, November 2, 2019

It is Saturday. I worked out with my trainer Eddy Goicolea yesterday afternoon and it's taking until after lunchtime today for my body to want to get going. It prompts me to write about bodies today and how you should think about your body. That is if you're planning to keep on going with your sex life.

I fell in the street Wednesday night after my grueling three hour Spanish class. I had taken my yoga class that morning and perhaps was a little more fatigued than usual. I caught my foot on a street tile and "bam" down on my hands and knees I went, books flying in all directions. I was walking with my friend Harry Baxter, who was quite concerned about my nearly 90 year old self going ass-over-teakettle in the street. I scrambled up and it seemed that I had only hit one knee rather badly. But it in no way interfered with my walking.

When I got home I discovered that I had only scraped my knee, and that not very severely. A large Band-Aid fitted over the scraped skin. My bones seem strong for my age. I fell over on my bicycle twice before I stopped riding it and both times my injuries were like this. Scraped skin and no bone problems.

I recount all this only because in my workout with my trainer he pointed out that certain exercises I regularly do are what keeps my leg bones strong. And the fairly minimal weight lifting I do with him keeps my arms and shoulders in place and firm.

I find my yoga classes are much more athletic than one might expect and I think these three times a week exercise activities are what keep my bones strong as well as my muscles. Which is only to advise you that if you do not have some kind of exercise pattern in your life you might easily fall and really break something. I know it's hard as I have many friends a good bit younger than myself who don't exercise much and once they pass sixty they are beginning to pile on weight and not get around very well.

My trainer told me that his father, who walks with a metal walker or a cane, was going to his backyard storeroom and slipped in mud. Falling, he couldn't get up and called out to his wife. This lady, who is my trainer's step-mother, came to her husband's rescue. Being a good bit overweight she too fell in the yard. Neither could get up. They laid in the mud for an hour before a neighbor pulled into his driveway and came to their aid when they called out. I couldn't help laughing and then thought of their situation. Without a neighbor they might have been sprawled in their backyard for some time. Perhaps overnight.

If you want to avoid sprawling in the backyard, or on a public sidewalk like me, you have to consider your fitness. The great corollary is that you are then bringing a trim and active body to your potential sexual confrontations.

I have been hesitant about bringing up the need for you to be existing in an active body. When I read the *New York Times* health columns and they repeatedly point out that people who walk a few blocks everyday are much healthier than those who don't, I'm pleased to read it. But I'm guessing that their bodies don't look much different.

When I see the women in my yoga class ranging between 68 and 75 I am much more encouraged. They have the trim bodies of women in their late 20s. They are all single, as widows or divorcees, and they spend evenings in jazz clubs and local theaters. A good friend from the class has gone online and now sees a 55 year old man who is dragging her into bed with great regularity. She married young and had quite a few children so this is her long-awaited dating period. She is certainly having a life quite different from most women as they approach 70. It is her fit and feminine body that is helping her greatly to have the romantic life she very much wishes to have.

The other subject that has been on my mind, as some of the people reading what I'm writing have been telling me, is that it isn't devoting enough time to sex itself. When you are sleeping regularly with someone and you enjoy it, you have to think a good bit about what the other person likes sexually. Yes, you are there to pursue what you like to do sexually; but there is also a pleasure to be gotten in making sure of the fulfillment of your partner, in knowing that the other person is having fulfilling sex also. There is a satisfaction for you in knowing that the other person has had the sexual experience they wanted to have. I think in early sexual experiences men plunge in, wrap up their sex activity in a jiffy and retreat, leaving the woman with little sexual gratification. This can have a big effect upon how one sex partner thinks about the other and the degree to which they look forward to more sexual contact. It's not something many married couples want to discuss but I think it's pretty common.

There is something quite entertaining in leading your sex partner off down lanes and byways they perhaps hadn't even thought of as possible or exciting. If you are the one with the imagination then you must lead the explorations. If you feel you need some coaching you can rent pornography and see if there are things being done that might interest you. Actually I think everyone is full of ideas once they get past the idea that sex is something bad. If it isn't harming someone else you are certainly entitled to explore whatever your body suggests it might like to do.

One last thing that has passed through my mind today is that you must keep fit not to be relegated as the years pass to the older category of "okay but not in our world." Don't let younger people relegate you to a category in which you do not belong.

Diary Comment Twenty-One

It will be a little difficult to comment upon the entry for a Saturday in November as it reprises many things that I have discussed at some length in my preceding comments.

My subconscious suggests that I bring up here a social tool that can draw another person closer to you and they will only rarely resist. You can read their palm. This is not as complex or difficult as you may think.

You read the palm that is not their writing hand. This will usually be their left hand. But occasionally you will come upon a lefthander and you will need to read their right palm.

Every palm has three major lines. The first one to consider is at the top of the palm. It begins on the right side immediately below the little finger and travels to the left. This is the HEART line. This line indicates the role of love, romance, and attachment play in this person's life. My own is a series of shortish interlaced lines that create a rather thick and long braided-looking line. This would indicate that there have been a number of romances that arrive, overlap, and disappear while a new line weaves onward. I cannot disagree with this interpretation of the line's meaning. In other hands this line may be only one single line. Or perhaps two or three. What is also important is its size and importance in relation to the other two lines. In my hand it is very dominant.

The second major line begins on the left side of the palm between the thumb and forefinger. Its beginning is linked to the third line, which descends towards the bottom of the hand. This second line is the HEAD line. This line in my hand is a single line, much smaller than the line above it, the HEART line. In my hand it is not dominant. It divides into two directions towards its ending in the direction of the right side of the palm. This may indicate going cuckoo or perhaps having a different point of view in the latter part of my life, which in fact is happening now towards the end of my ninth decade on this planet. Clearly my HEART line plays a much more important role in my life than my HEAD line. I have no argument. I have always made my decisions based on how I feel than what rationality might dictate.

The third major line that descends to the bottom of our palm is your LIFE line. It should always be made clear when reading someone else's palm that the length of the LIFE line has no connection to the length of one's life. However it may indicate the passage of someone's life. I have a number of short lines crossing my LIFE line in its upper length. This could well indicate the many changes of directions my life has taken. I have been a ballet dancer, naval officer, an advertising writer, an author of many books, and have returned to the cabaret stage.

Toward the lower area it divides and since I now am both a writer and a cabaret performer this may be an indication of that in my life.

This is all you really need to know to tackle reading someone else's palm. It can be a great deal more complex but for a little social tete-a-tete this is quite enough knowledge. HEART at top, HEAD in the middle, LIFE at the bottom.

Using a tool like this you can become much more of a close friend, perhaps more of an intimate companion. Or perhaps you can more quickly see that this person is not going to develop into some kind of romantic partner. The excellent aspect of this interaction is they will certainly enjoy being the center of attention and will reveal a great many things about themselves, even if denying that what you are perceiving is true.

In doing this with others I will point out that I rarely have had anyone disagree a great deal at what I was discovering in their palm and it has certainly heightened the intimacy between us a great deal and rapidly.

Monday, November 4, 2019

It's Monday and I want to record here something I read excerpted from a book review. The author Elizabeth Strout has written a book called "Olive Again." Evidently this is a follow up to her book "Olive Kitteridge," which was also made into a TV series.

Her character is being discussed and the author says, "There's a myth out there that when somebody reaches a certain age, they stop growing. I don't think that's true. I think until the last breath people are continuing to grow."

I think the energy within us that makes the difference between our being dead and our being alive is always there and is always prompting both our bodies and our minds to find out more about this place in which we find ourselves. On this ball whirling through space. Here we are, some kind of development from animals that once went from wearing fur to having little farms and have rather rapidly in the past few centuries arrived at this electronics-dominated environment. It appears to me that the main impediment in our continuing growth is ourselves. We involve ourselves with other people for security. Or work for companies that dangle security at the end of long and boring days. We think of the things we would like to do as being only fantasies. Experiences and exploration are not our goals nor do we really consider fulfillment as a goal as it is rarely brought to our attention by those around us.

I read only today that the president of our country has a female religious advisor whose Protestant subdivision has a spiritual goal of "health and wealth." All you have to do is ask yourself if you would like to be like the very wealthy billionaires who are influencing our world in so many ways. They are not a very appealing lot. Certainly not in the sexual category.

Diary Comment Twenty-Two

Another diary entry from November encourages the reader to pursue life goals with the knowledge that we continue to grow throughout our lives. Things that we may have wanted when younger change as we pass through our years here aboard planet Earth.

This is all very much directed to the reader to encourage the pursuit of a fulfilling life. What I would like to add here is further encouragement in the pursuit of a private life as well as a public life.

I have just been reading a collection of quotes from a wide variety of sources as to aspects of an emotional life. I particularly liked one from Lord Byron. His lifetime was 1788 to 1824. You may know little about this famous lover and writer but he left England to live in Italy as he felt the English too restrictive to pass his life among them. This is what he wrote about love.

"His <u>voice</u> first attracted my attention. His <u>countenance</u> fixed it, and his <u>manners</u> attached me to him forever."

After we clarify in our minds that "countenance" is the period's description of the face and that "manners" is reference to someone's style of interaction, we can understand his expression of drawing someone into your ambience and retaining them there.

By "F***able" in the title of this book there has always been the intention of how one may draw someone into a completely personal interaction with yourself. It was never intended to be a guidebook on how to make bamboola.

In that we always know there is one person on top, another person on top, standing, kneeling, lying on the floor, etc., etc., etc., which hardly need describing if you've been around a few years. This book is intended to encourage you to believe you can always be fascinating. Lord Byron's quote encouraged me to believe that I am right in my encouraging you forward with your life. I hope that you have found the same thing reading my book.

Friday, May 1, 2020

A very unusual phone call today. A man called. He had originally been from my hometown. He had met me when he was 14. His aunt was a next-door neighbor to my mother and when he was visiting her she had taken him next door to meet me. That was what he told me. Since I am now 90 years old and he is 80, I would have been 24. I was a junior officer in the U.S. Navy at this time so it ws unlikely I would have been visiting my mother at that time.

However, I was discharged from the Navy shortly after my 25th birthday so perhaps he was off a bit. He had been very impressed with me and had never forgotten me. My opinion of myself has never included being impressive to anyone when I was that age as I was leaving the Navy and traveling on to New York to launch some kind of career, some kind of life. I was very unsure of myself at that time.

He talked at some length and explained that he was a younger brother of a classmate of mine who was from a farm family in the country near my hometown. His family were very firmly attached to their farming background. His meeting me evidently gave him the impetus to plan to not return to the farm after his high school graduation or even after his college graduation. He began to think of a life that might be possible removed from his family background. He would be the first in his family to do so since their early pioneer arrival in this part of the country.

He had somehow gotten my current phone number to verify if I was indeed the person he had met so long ago. He had gotten the number from the only classmate of mine in my hometown with whom I still remained in contact. His explanation as to how he had tracked down this person wasn't really explained. He was doing all this, he said, because a nephew had contacted him and wanted the many books I've written. This would make sense. Yet somehow I got the feeling that the nephew was an imaginary reason for his rediscovering me.

He explained that his departure from our hometown had led to a career in banking throughout our home state and he currently lives in retirement in a nearby city. I told him I would send him a few books, including my autobiography which would perhaps add to his information about our shared experiences in and around this small old place where we both had begun our lives.

Friday, May 7, 2020

I received another phone call from my new friend today. He had received my books and seemed quite excited about reading them. This is always a pleasure for a writer to hear. We will see how all of this transpires and unfolds.

Afterword

Yesterday morning I awoke thinking and feeling how much I missed and needed the one with whom I am emotionally involved.

I called him where he lives in a foreign country and he said, "I felt the same thing today. I realized how much you are part of my life. I thought of you and my body began to shake and the hair on my arms stood up."

I tell you this from my position in my 90th year. If someone more than half a century younger than yourself can say this, this book is not a needless fantasy. It is my reaching out to my readers to plunge forward with their lives, no matter what their age may be. No matter what may look like a sensible direction in the years ahead. Our lives are to be lived. Please do. You will never regret it.

A NOTE FROM THE AUTHOR

If you'd like to reach me for any reason, or like to be added to my mailing list, send an email—I'd love to hear from you. It would also be nice if you left a review on the page where you got this book. That helps potential readers know what you think! And thank you.

david@davidleddick.net

Turn the page to see
Several Other Titles by David Leddick
Available at Amazon online stores worldwide

MY WORST DATE

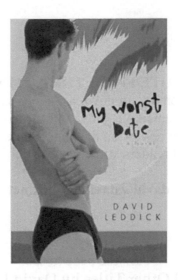

From the outside, Hugo wouldn't strike anyone as remarkable. In fact, he is much the same as any other sixteen-year-old in South Beach, Miami. He lives with his single mother, hangs out with his best friend, spends time at the beach, is secretly seeing someone his mother definitely wouldn't approve of him seeing, and, while he finishes high school, he is working a part-time job to save money for college.

But Hugo is anything but a typical sixteen-year-old. His part-time job is not at the local pizza place like he told his mother, but rather at a local gay club, where he works as a go-go boy. And the person he is seeing on the sly is a much older man, one Glenn Elliot Paul, whom Hugo met when he walked into his mother's real estate office. And to make it that much worse, Glenn is also dating Hugo's mother.

2B OR NOT 2B

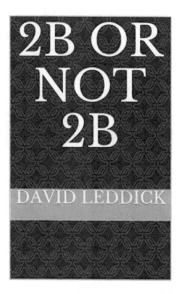

Muriel Hopewell is that new kind of woman: in the Boomer generation, living in a retirement community, still interested in romance. She lives in apartment 2A. She connects with the man living in 2C, who may not be quite who he seems. Between them is apartment 2B, whose occupants seem to die too rapidly, too mysteriously. What's going on? Muriel wants to find out. So will you.

THE SEX SQUAD

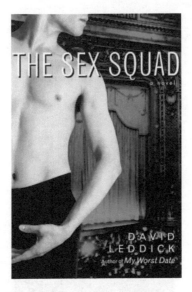

In the 1950's, seventeen-year old Harry Potter moves to New York's Greenwich Village to pursue a career as a ballet dancer. Professionally, he finds a place as a chorus dancer at the old Metropolitan Opera house and becomes a member of the "Sex Squad" -- those chorus dancers well-built enough to carry off the skimpy costumes in *Aida*.

Personally, he quickly becomes the focal point in a tempestuous, complicated love triangle with two of his fellow dancers. Torn between passion and his true love--dancing--Harry must come to a decision about whom he loves, who he is, and what he is willing to sacrifice for the world of ballet.

LOVE IN THE LOIRE

"Love in the Loire" continues the story of teen-ager Hugo Bianchi, who in David Leddick's novel "My Worst Date" has an affair with his mother's boyfriend. Now he's doing summer theater in the Loire Valley in France and his mother arrives for a visit with the boyfriend. There is much distraction with Broadway celebrities and sexy locals mixing it up. Hugo gets a chance to hit the big time and also to find true love. He learns a lot. So will you.

AHEAD OF THE CROWD - VOL. 1
Travels Around the World: 1963-2017 In 3 Volumes

Beginning in 1963, David Leddick traveled alone as he didn't want to share his voyages with a fellow American who would make too easy to stay in his U.S.A. shell looking out.

No, he went by himself. He was lonely and alone. But then he felt truly absorbed into the country he visited. Each week he wrote long letters home to his mother with his travels and impressions very fully detailed. After her death he found she had saved all these communications.

He returned to Europe the following year and then during the rest of the decade first went to the South Pacific. He had served there during his duty in the Navy and there were places he had always wanted to visit but hadn't.

Now he did. Tahiti, Fiji and more.

Then over the years off to Russia, Sardinia, Mardi Gras in New Orleans, China, Africa and much more, some of them places few Americans had visited at the time.

AHEAD OF THE CROWD - VOL. 1
Travels Around the World: 1963-2017 In 3 Volumes

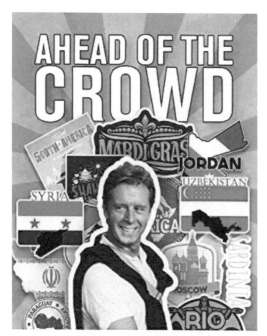

AHEAD OF THE CROWD - VOL. 2
Travels Around the World: 1963-2017 In 3 Volumes

"It was interesting to see Leddick's take on Paris in the 1960s. That's when air travel to Europe was just getting started." – Leanne Rylander, Liverpool

"When the author went to a lot of these places, Americans were few and far between—a remarkable journey." –Jerry Adams, Atlanta

"He certainly offers a fresh perspective on the exotic places he made it to. Places I can only hope I to visit—someday." – Philip Runmeade, Baltimore

David Leddick made his first international trip from the United States in 1963. He went to London, Paris and the major cities of Italy. In the next two decades he branched out from Europe to cross the vastness of a Russia that had seen almost no outsiders. Then, with a Zen study group, he traveled for a month through a China that was so closed off by its insular Communist regime that the inhabitants had seen no tourists at all. This period of Leddick's travels finished with a deep plunge into the depths of Africa on an extended safari. His fascinating exploration of the Earth, this globe on which he was traveling through space, had begun.

AHEAD OF THE CROWD - VOL. 2
Travels Around the World: 1963-2017 In 3 Volumes

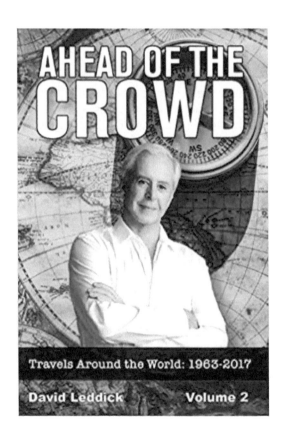

AHEAD OF THE CROWD - VOL. 3
Travels Around the World: 1963-2017 In 3 Volumes

In another decade of travel well into the 21st Century David Leddick explored South America more fully, even establishing a residence In Montevideo, capital of the tiny country Uruguay wedged between Argentina to the south and vast Brazil to the north.

After renovating his 1890s house in the old quarter of Montevideo, he began to explore Brazil, beginning with Rio de Janeiro, following up with a voyage to Sao Paulo.

He interspersed these visits with journeys to Naples in Italy, a favored city. He added to this several sidetrips to nearby glamorous Capri, the Isle where many international travelers go regularly.

Returns to South America led to visits to Curacao, Cancun, and Lima. There were added several sidetrips to Panama, squarely between the north and south continents. He now lives very much midway between the North and South Americas in Miami Beach, Florida.

AHEAD OF THE CROWD - VOL. 3
Travels Around the World: 1963-2017 In 3 Volumes

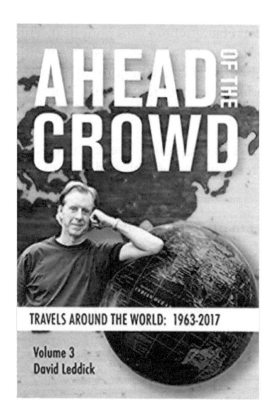

A NOTE FROM THE AUTHOR

If you enjoyed this book, please take a moment to leave a review on the website where you bought it. This would be a great favor to me. Honest reviews let potential readers discover my books. This is a major way in which all writers find new readers. Your review is MUCH more helpful than you might think.

And if you'd like to drop me a line, by all means, please do. I answer each email personally, and love to hear from my readers.

Email – david@davidleddick.net

Made in United States
Troutdale, OR
01/31/2024

17330653R00076